ENTREPRENUMBERS

ENTREPRENUMBERS

THE SURPRISINGLY SIMPLE PATH
TO FINANCIAL CLARITY

SPENCER SHEININ, CPA, CA

LIONCREST
PUBLISHING

ENTREPRENUMBERS

The Surprisingly Simple Path to Financial Clarity

ISBN   978-1-5445-0419-3 *Hardcover*
       978-1-5445-0418-6 *Paperback*
       978-1-5445-0417-9 *Ebook*

CONTENTS

INTRODUCTION

THIS IS NOT AN ACCOUNTING LESSON!

I drove to work feeling nauseous every morning.

The feeling only intensified when I walked into the office—into my own personal version of *Groundhog Day*. Every audit was the same; none of it was interesting or challenging. I'd get out my green pen, tick off a bunch of receipts, and repeat with the next stack. The future offered no relief from the monotony.

There was no way around it: I hated accounting.

OK, maybe I didn't hate accounting. I hated aspects of accounting, like auditing, bookkeeping, and reconciliations—just about anything routine and recurring. On second thought, I *did* hate accounting.

I'd never meant to get into accounting in the first place. During my last year of university, I needed a plan for after graduation. My father suggested I look into the CA (now CPA) program. The idea didn't sound half bad. I'd seen how successful he'd become with his own tax practice, and I'd be working while I did a second degree, which sounded way better than more school with no work experience.

The accounting program consisted of a mix of exams and "article" time in an accredited accounting firm. The word "article" is derived from a Latin term meaning "low-paid grunt work." Back then everything was manual. During my first year, we only had two computers for the entire floor, which had to be signed out and wheeled back to my desk. A lot of the work involved printing accounting reports, pulling invoices from a pile of boxes, and literally ticking them off one at a time. Equally as stimulating was the task of manually adding up columns on reports to make sure they were calculated properly.

Everything about the accounting program sucked, but quitting was never an option. So I put my head down, worked hard, and, a few years later, got my CA.

The question was, *what next?* Accounting certainly wasn't my calling. I disliked the work, and the path to accounting partner didn't inspire me—in fact, it made me feel worse.

Fresh degree or not, my accounting career was over before it started.

I went into investment banking next, again on the advice of my father. It was *Groundhog Day* all over again. One of my core duties as an analyst was creating "comp analyses," which involved comparing financial statements from several public companies within the same industry to assess value. As a junior analyst, that meant pulling a bunch of companies' quarterly and annual reports—all manual labor in the early days of the internet—followed by hours of entering them into Excel spreadsheets, one line at a time. While the analysis itself was interesting (I was regularly surprised at the reasons why some companies were valued so differently than others in the public markets), the grunt work of putting them together was just as nauseating as ticking off receipts with a green pen during an audit.[1]

The other main task was building financial models. These were complex Excel workbooks where we modeled the financial future of a company based on a set of changing assumptions. While I actually enjoyed the process of building a model, I regularly worked until two or three o'clock in the morning because of the nature of M&A (mergers and acquisitions) deadlines. Further, the models were so sensitive and complex that they ran several Excel worksheets

---

[1] Note: My dad gives great advice and has been the biggest supporter of my career. Just because I didn't love accounting or investment banking, didn't mean it was bad advice!

deep. One little mistake could "#REF out" your model (read: completely break it) and force you to go cell by cell looking through each formula for the error.

A few months of this, and I felt that nauseous feeling creeping back in. Within a year I knew I had to make another change.

ADVENTURES IN ENTREPRENEURSHIP

As much as the work in my early days in the financial world bored me, the skills I developed during that period set the foundation for my future. Both accounting and investment banking taught me how to read between the lines and uncover the stories buried deep inside financial statements. I intuitively know when something is wrong and when the relationships are out of whack.

So, at the ripe old age of twenty-six, I jumped into entrepreneurship with both feet. I fanaticized about the lifestyle. I'd be my own boss, I'd have all the money and free time I could handle, and I'd be able to pursue my passion for endurance sports without any worries.

Spoiler alert: it was ridiculously harder than expected and I made every mistake imaginable along the way.

All the entrepreneurs reading this book know exactly what

I'm talking about. For the next decade, I was constantly surprised at just how much I had to learn. Every time I felt like I made progress and maybe even mastered some aspect of business, I discovered the need for three more critical skills—each of which I completely sucked at. Since my experiences in those businesses directly led to my writing this book, it's worth taking just a moment to explore that journey.

My first business was a skincare manufacturing company. I didn't have a particular interest in skincare, but a friend of mine asked if I wanted to go into business with him. We had totally different skillsets but had the same vision, the same values, and the same work ethic. I had a ton of schooling and financial background. He had no schooling and a ton of practical experience and sales skills. Perfect!

We looked at a few opportunities and after a few months zeroed in on a manufacturing business. During our first due-diligence tour of the company's production floor, I stood silently watching lip balm roll off the end of the production line. I thought all we'd have to do is work hard, outperform the competition, and we'd be set. My partner was thinking the exact same thing. We put in our bid and ultimately bought the business. I'd been involved in several acquisitions, so the analysis and financing (over 90 percent of the acquisition cost) was relatively easy. I managed the operational and financial side of the business while my partner handled sales and marketing. Over the next ten-plus years, we grew the business from about $2.5 million to just over $10 million in revenue, becoming the largest manufacturer of our type in our region.

About eight years into my work at the skincare manufacturing company, I was invited to become a partner in two other businesses. The first was a construction company owned by my existing partner; the other was a family business in public refrigerated warehousing (a.k.a., cold storage). While I was aware I might be taking on too much, by this point I had nearly a decade of experience owning and growing the skincare company. I was confident my skills were relevant in the other businesses and also confident I could add value to both.

After the requisite legal work, I had stakes in three $10 million-plus businesses with over three hundred employees between them, taking a big step toward my vision of becoming a mini-Warren Buffet. Things were running smoothly on all fronts, and we began lining up professional management teams in each business in order to extract ourselves from day-to-day operations and focus on new acquisition opportunities.

TOO GOOD TO BE TRUE

Did I have some good luck to get to this point? Absolutely.

I'd found myself in the right markets at the right time—and I'd done so during a period of prosperity and economic growth. These were important factors because, if I'm being honest, I didn't have all the skills I really needed and was certainly lacking experience. That said, I also worked my ass off to learn what I needed to know and make sure we were successful.

Unlike my days as an accountant, I was eager to get in to work every (read: most) day(s). I woke up early. I regularly drove to work before the sun came up. I was usually the first person to arrive in the office (though the manufacturing team was always there before me) and often the last person to leave. I was happy to do it. Good luck aside, I poured my blood, sweat, and tears into each of my companies, and I was thrilled to see how far we had come after a decade-plus of grinding it out.

Then 2008 happened.

Like a lot of businesses, we found ourselves on the defensive. Instead of advancing my vision of acquiring more businesses, reality set in, and I ended up back in the weeds, grinding it out during the biggest (pretty much only) recession I'd ever experienced.

Together with my partners, I made a few strategic moves in response. First, we sold the cold storage business to a private equity (PE) firm that was "rolling up" the industry—in other words, they were buying up independent companies with the goal of turning into a mega-company. We had decent interest in the company as there were a number of different PE firms competing in the roll-up. Given the business climate at the time, both the timing and the money felt right. While we didn't do quite as well as we would have liked, we did a lot better than we could have in the post-2008 world.

Second, my other partner and I decided to split our businesses—he'd take the construction business, which was his to begin with, and I'd take the skincare company. It was an amicable split (we're still friends today), and we decided the split was best for both of us. Our reasoning was simple. I was brought into the construction business to help transition my partner out of the day-to-day operations by implementing processes and procedures to make him redundant. What I discovered was that he *was* the competitive advantage of the company, and there was no way to transition him out without killing the business. He has skills and abilities beyond anything I've ever seen—magical, telepathic skills when it comes to designing and building a house. I would put him up against the best custom home builders in the country and have no doubt he'd come out on top. Once we realized that he was the heart and soul of that business, it made sense for me to exit.

We decided I'd focus exclusively on the skincare business,

while my partner stayed with construction. That's how we weathered the financial storm and eventually stabilized. My accounting background saved my ass many times in this regard. If I hadn't had the knowledge that I did, I would have been completely screwed in the post-2008 world. I could see the story our financials were telling us—the early warning signs that many other business owners didn't—and I was able to pivot and set priorities accordingly.

As business returned to normal over the next few years, I had some time to reflect on our long-term prospects. I realized that while things were better for the moment, there were other challenges on the horizon, a lot of them. We were getting squeezed between giant suppliers and giant customers, being regulated to death (we had *eight* regulatory audits in 2014) and undercut by commoditized competitors with a geographic advantage.

I could see that we weren't structured for long-term success, and I knew that I wasn't the person to lead the business through those challenges. More importantly, I didn't believe in the business anymore and had been losing my passion for it over the past few years. When new challenges came at me, I didn't have the energy or desire to fight back. So, I made the hard decision to exit. I sold the assets to a large competitor out East who integrated our business into their facility. Despite no longer being passionate about it, after nearly fifteen years in the business, I felt tremendously conflicted the day I locked the door the last time.

IS THIS WHAT A MIDLIFE CRISIS LOOKS LIKE?

At the age of forty, I turned the page on my initial fifteen-year adventure in entrepreneurship. As I reflected on my career to that point, I was proud of what we'd accomplished, though I wasn't blind to my shortcomings either. Less than 7 percent of businesses get to be $1 million in revenue or more, and only around 1 percent of businesses get to be $10 million or more.[2] I'd crossed that threshold with three different businesses, managing over three hundred employees in total. At the same time, I'd gone in completely naïve to how challenging running a business really was; and no matter how hard I worked, there were competitors out there working just as hard or harder.

I had no idea what my next step would be. This time, instead of rushing into the first opportunity that came my way, I resolved to take a year off, define what I wanted to do and, more importantly, what I *didn't* want to do, and take it from there.

---

2   "US Business Firmographics—Company Size | NAICS Association," NAICS Association, 2019, https://www.naics.com/business-lists/counts-by-company-size/.

PROBLEMS IN STARTUP LAND

I can't sit still for long. To keep myself occupied, I did a bit of angel investing and advising a few local tech startups. Without fail, as soon as they learned about my financial background, they asked me to join their company as fractional CFO, bringing credibility to their company while handling the numbers side of things. While I wasn't looking for this kind of role, I had some spare time and figured I could help. So, I somewhat begrudgingly agreed to take that role with a few different companies.

At one company, I knew we had a problem after my first conversation with the bookkeeper. Peggy worked hard and was nice enough, but it was painfully obvious she didn't know what she was doing. The questions she asked were shockingly simple—below accounting 101 simple—and I couldn't get the most basic reports or information from her.

I brought my concerns to our energetic young CEO and asked what he thought of Peggy's work. He told me that she'd been recommended by a friend who said she was amazing.

"Do *you* think she's amazing?" I asked.

"I have no idea. I'm just trusting what my friend said."

I told him the truth: Peggy was not, in fact, amazing. Even

more alarming was that she'd coasted for over a year on her reputation without knowing even basic accounting principles.

"Oh," he said. "Now what?"

THE ENTREPRENEUR'S DILEMMA

My conversation with this entrepreneur helped me realize the real problem: **Entrepreneurs' financial blind spots run *way* deeper than I thought.**

The problem wasn't that our CEO had hired a bad bookkeeper. It was that he had no clue what a good bookkeeper even was. When it came to understanding his company's books, he didn't really know much. That's not a poke or an insult. He'd been avoiding his books and was completely oblivious to anything related to his numbers. He didn't know the difference between good books and a hot mess. He had no idea what to ask of his bookkeeper, how to direct her work, and, worst of all, he had no understanding of how to use the financial information he *was* given. Even if the information was accurate—which it wasn't—he would have been lost.

That experience wasn't unique. At virtually every company I advised or joined as CFO during my "year off," the pattern repeated itself:

1. The books were usually a complete mess, the entrepreneurs didn't know what to ask for, the bookkeepers weren't up to the task, and no one was putting in basic procedures for even the most simplistic financial oversight.
2. Even if the bookkeeper was doing a good job, they had no idea how to deliver it to the entrepreneur in a way they understood. It was always "Here are your financials," and the entrepreneur promptly tucked them in a pile marked "to review." After a few months, the oldest and still-untouched financials would be tossed, making way for the next set.

The reality is that most entrepreneurs simply don't speak accounting. They hate the very idea of it—even more than I did when I was doing my CA. Maybe they don't get nauseous thinking about it like I did, but that's probably because they avoid it altogether.

I get it. Being an entrepreneur is a lot harder than it looks, and way harder than non-entrepreneurs could ever imagine. There are a million things going on. There are always issues to sort out, demands on time, and ongoing staff issues. The list is unending. Hence the avoidance.

I was frustrated. I wanted to help, but I was stuck between bookkeepers that couldn't deliver the basics and entrepreneurs who desperately needed help understanding what the numbers were trying to tell them.

MY AHA MOMENT

Aha moments never happen when you're expecting them. Mine came while listening to a speaker named Alan Miltz at an Entrepreneurs' Organization (EO) event in Vancouver.

Alan Miltz is nothing short of brilliant. The Australian teaches entrepreneurs how banks analyze their books using a series of financial ratios. He's the perfect speaker on the subject, considering that he created the systems that some 450 banks use for this exact purpose.

As brilliant as Alan is, he speaks fast and expects the audience to keep up. I had to be completely focused to follow what he was saying. For the entrepreneurs in the room without a financial background, a lot of the session was going right over their heads.

About halfway through the talk, he was walking us through one of his signature formulas when, in an innocent slip-up, he gave the wrong answer.

I raised my hand. "Pardon me, Alan, shouldn't the answer be 2.44 instead of 2.2?"

"Oh, you're right," he said. "Good catch."

Those who were struggling to keep up burst out laughing, surprised to see that I was following along well enough to *correct* him. After the talk, one of the entrepreneurs whom I'd known for a few years came up to me to say hi. We exchanged pleasantries and had a little laugh about my moment with Alan. Then he said, "Hey, can you put this process into place in my business?"

That was my aha moment.

The problem I saw in startup land wasn't unique to startups. Even seasoned entrepreneurs with teams of ten, twenty, or even fifty-plus employees struggle with financial literacy.

Alan's talk had been amazing. Every entrepreneur in the room recognized its importance, but many didn't have the basics in place enough to implement it in their own business. Many of them didn't even know where to get started. I did, and I knew I could help others put those processes into action. Of course, we just had to get their basic accounting dialed in first.[3]

Both my life as a CPA/investment banker and my life as an entrepreneur came full circle in that moment. I realized I could be the bridge between these two worlds: the person who could take advanced accounting and finance practices and make them easily accessible and totally intuitive to

---

3   Let me be clear: Alan's "Power of One" is a great tool for businesses that have the basics in place and a level of sophistication to leverage the tool. What we'll be talking about in this book is for those who don't know where to get started or whose books are a mess (sometimes/often/ usually both).

entrepreneurs depending on them for their businesses to succeed.

Already my mind was reeling with possibilities. However, the start of a new idea and the opportunity to implement it isn't always linear.

SERENDIPITY STRIKES

A few days later, I was on the phone with Shannon, my former director of sales from the skincare company. I was venting about my situation because she's always been awesome at helping me work through issues. "I've got all these companies asking me to be their CFO, and I see the gap that needs to be filled, but I can't get the information I need out of them because none of them have the basics in place. I don't want to jump in as bookkeeper and controller too, and I don't have the skills for it anyway. If only I had Anna. I could put her into all of these companies and get them cleaned up in no time."

Anna had been my controller at the skincare company for over ten years. She was amazing—not Peggy amazing, but *amazing* amazing. She knew how to manage a bookkeeper, how to implement processes and procedures, and how to deliver meaningful information so I could do my thing as CFO.

"Have you talked to Anna recently?" Shannon asked. "Because she's unhappy where she is right now."

I laughed. "No, I hadn't even thought of it."

I called Anna the next day. "Don't quit your day job," I said, "but here's what I'm thinking."

Two weeks later, Anna called me back. "I just quit my job. Let's do it."

"OK," I said. "I guess we're doing this!" That was the start of Shift Financial Insights (my current company), and we took on our first few clients handling the role of bookkeeper, controller, and CFO with the promise to make accounting *not suck* for entrepreneurs.

THE ROAD TO CLARITY AND SIMPLICITY

At this point you may be wondering, "This guy said he *hates* accounting. So why did he start an accounting firm?"

Great question.

I love working with entrepreneurs. I love the enthusiasm they bring to their work. So much so that I've made it our mission to **help entrepreneurs through their financial blind spots so they can change the world**. I also love the power of the stories buried inside the financial. I just don't want to do the *actual* accounting.

If I were doing the accounting myself, I'd still be waking up with that pit in my stomach every day. Fortunately, I have a team who *loves* doing accounting work, and because of my unique background, I have the privilege of creating a bridge between the accounting world and the entrepreneurial world.

That's my passion—and that's why I can own an outsourced accounting firm now.

I began Shift Financial because I saw a pressing need in the business world. Entrepreneurs and accountants don't know how to talk to each other or understand each other's needs. Once I saw the problem, I realized I could provide a path forward for entrepreneurs by creating clarity and simplicity around their books.

I wrote this book to further that mission.

I know firsthand how frustrating accounting can be. It was my job—a job that left me feeling nauseous every single day. I also know firsthand how difficult being an entrepreneur can be—I've had a lot of stress-filled sleepless nights. I've seen how hard it can be to get the information you need from your accounting team, *and I know what to ask for*. I can only imagine how much harder it is for the many, many entrepreneurs out there who aren't numbers-minded and don't have the financial background I have.

Imagine how much better your business would be if you understood with perfect clarity all of the stories buried inside your financial statements and you could make decisions based on sound financial data, not just a hunch. Also imagine if you could do that *intuitively* and *quickly*, **without having to dig into the details of your financial statements.** After the following chapters, you won't have to imagine anymore.

CALLING ALL ENTREPRENEURS

This book is for entrepreneurs who are frustrated, stuck, embarrassed, annoyed, or avoiding their books.

It's for all the entrepreneurs who wake up every morning (if they even fell asleep at all) with a sinking feeling in their stomachs. Entrepreneurs who don't "get" their numbers and are uncertain where to start or what questions to ask. Finally, this book is for all the entrepreneurs who know they need something better than what they've got, but who can't afford a CFO or a controller in addition to their bookkeeper.[4]

---

4   If you're one of the lucky, more established entrepreneurs who can afford a fully staffed accounting team, I promise you'll find some useful tips and strategies in this book. But it wasn't written specifically for you.

Let me be very clear: ***this is not an accounting lesson***. I am not going to teach you about accounting or even how to read your financial statements. Instead, I will teach you how to delegate tasks to your bookkeeper/accounting team[5] and how to instruct them to get you the *right* information, at the *right* time, and, most importantly, in a format that works for you (intuitive with no accounting jargon).

It doesn't matter where in the world you live or operate. The principles in this book still apply to you. While there are subtle differences in accounting rules between, say, the United States, Canada, Australia, and a developing country, we're talking about making the data easy for you to understand. If you've taken care to hire and properly direct a qualified accounting team, they will be able to help you regardless of the region or jurisdiction you live in. If you don't have a strong team, we have some suggestions for you too.

With these tools, you can begin to build the rock-solid, bulletproof accounting department you've always wanted, but never knew how to create.

To help you on that journey, I've set the book up in four parts:

- **Part 1** will give you a big-picture look at common chal-

---

5   For the purposes of this book, we will use the terms "accountant" and "bookkeeper" interchangeably. If we're not talking about your internal accounting team, we'll say "external accountant" or specifically define it otherwise.

lenges facing all small businesses, the gaps and blind spots you likely have in your own business, and a first crack at what an awesome alternative could look like for you.

- **Part 2** dives into the key levers facing **all** businesses. Understanding these levers will help simplify your financial world and add context to the learnings in the rest of this book.
- **Part 3** is a deep dive into the gold-standard monthly reporting package, including how to make it simple, intuitive, and quick for you to use and understand. Once you've implemented this package, you'll have everything you need to truly drive the best decisions for your business.
- **Part 4** introduces the Hygiene Roadmap. Think of this as the basics of a healthy accounting department—how to direct your team to ensure that they are doing what they need to be doing daily, weekly, monthly, quarterly, and annually to make sure your books are in top shape.

I'm also including informational sidebars for your accounting team, just like the one that follows. There's no need for you to worry about those gray boxes addressed to accountants—they're just shop talk for us weenie accountants (but keep your eyes out for the gray boxes addressed to Entrepreneurs). Feel free to skip them and keep reading ahead.

I'll see you in chapter 1.

TO ALL THE BOOKKEEPERS AND
ACCOUNTANTS READING THIS BOOK

The entrepreneur you work for probably heard about this book from a talk I gave or on recommendation from a friend. Now, they've given it to you to read. While they're off watching TED Talks and doing other entrepreneurial things, I have a few words I'd like to share with you.

First, I will make fun of accountants all throughout this book. Don't worry, I'm an accountant too, so I'm just making fun of myself. This book is for you as much as it is for the entrepreneurs. It may not be addressed to you, and it's certainly not written in our supersecret accounting language, but it will help you better understand how entrepreneurs think and what they really need because they don't know how to explain it to you.

Second, accounting is changing. You need to learn how to change with the times or you'll be out of a job–especially if you're a bookkeeper. Think Blockbuster Video vs. Netflix. Accounting is being disrupted as much as the delivery of video content has been. Those who can learn from and implement the practices I've outlined in this book will be tomorrow's accounting heroes–and, let's face it, it's much more fun to be the boss's best friend than the butt of endless "weenie accountant" jokes. I know. I've heard them all.

You have an opportunity and an obligation here. As an industry, I believe we have largely failed our entrepreneurs, particularly those with under $10 million in revenue. We have been handing them financial statements in our language, the language we went to school for several years to learn, expecting them to know what to do with it. They don't, and they never will. Stop expecting them to speak your language, and learn to start speaking theirs!

If you're struggling to communicate important financial information to your entrepreneur, this book will help you understand why.

I'm fluent in both accountant-speak and entrepreneur-speak. I know how hard it can be to convey important financial information to entrepreneurs, and I'm with you on this journey to help you speak their language and make you more effective in your job. As you read along, pay attention to the language I use to disarm and empower them, so you can master it yourself. Fewer accounting words, fewer reports. More common language, more intuitive information, more data visualization (a.k.a. charts). Then, come find me in sidebars like this one, where I'll share some tips specifically designed to help you up your game.

PART 1

BETTER BOOKS, BETTER BUSINESS

Business is a dogfight.

In October 2000, boxers Mark Porter and Danny Williams faced off for the Commonwealth belt. In the sixth round with just under three minutes left, Williams threw a right hook that dislocated his shoulder. His corner didn't throw in the towel—he kept fighting with his non-dominant arm instead.

I don't know about you, but my non-dominant arm is about as strong as a wet noodle (remember, I'm an accountant). Williams's was certainly stronger than mine, but still that didn't change the fact that he was in a professional boxing match using only one arm. Somehow he fought on, evading enough of Porter's punches to stay in the fight.

Then, with about a minute left on the clock, Williams stepped into a left hook and knocked Porter to the ground. Porter got up, but Williams knocked him down again, winning by knockout—dislocated arm and all.

In many ways, being an entrepreneur is a lot like being a boxer. Your competitors want to beat you up—they want to *win*—and they will use whatever advantage they have. Every day you're in the fight of your life. If you're stepping into the ring with a dislocated arm, what do you think your odds are of winning? In the history of boxing, I suspect it's only happened once. To put it mildly, the odds aren't in your favor.

Any day that you go up against your competitors without a clear understanding of your books is like fighting with one arm, hoping to connect with a left hook—your path to success is narrow at best. A key ingredient your competitor needs to beat you is a better understanding of their numbers and the key financial issues facing their business. If they have that, they're going to win 99 percent of the time. Sure, you still have that rare chance of coming out on top, like Williams, but is that really a risk you want to take?

It's time to even the match. In part 1, I'm going to teach you why you showed up to the ring with only one arm and how to pop your arm back into its socket so you can get back in the ring and start taking charge of your books.

CHAPTER 1

———

CRISIS MODE

HOW DID I GET HERE?

As an entrepreneur, you're probably well acquainted with crisis mode. Maybe you're even in crisis mode now? Nothing seems to be going right. Customers aren't happy. Suppliers are calling for payment, even threatening to cut you off. Every time you turn around, there's another surprise waiting for you (and not the good kind). At some point during crisis mode, you inevitably ask yourself, "How did I get in this mess?"

Here's the most likely reason: You started, bought, inherited, or somehow else ended up owning your business. Regardless of how you've come to own it, you're not from a financial background. So, you handed off your books to someone else—a family member, family friend, or, if you're lucky, a part-time bookkeeper. You're stoked not having to deal with anything accounting and finance, so you turn in your receipts (maybe) and then you run away, believing that everything is going to be just fine and your accounting is handled. One hundred percent of your attention goes into sales and/or operations.

But as the business grows and becomes more complex, you start to notice some things aren't quite right. A couple of invoices go out wrong. Some reports you request from your bookkeeper seem to never come, or if they actually *do* come, you *know* something isn't right.

But you hate accounting so much that the perceived pain of actually *fixing* these accounting issues is much greater than the pain of living with the errors. Fixing it means diving headfirst into your accounting department—literally the last thing in the world you want to do—so you find yourself in *avoidance mode*. You avoid the problem, pretend like everything will be fine, and soldier on.

Your business continues to grow, which is great, but so does the complexity. The few errors you initially noticed turn into daily issues. You realize that the "small" problems you were avoiding before are compounding into huge problems. Not only are you not getting *any* good information; you're flying completely blind and not able to make any decisions, finding yourself squarely in *crisis mode*. You're no doubt intimately acquainted with the language of crisis mode:

"What do you mean we don't have enough in the bank account for payroll this week?"

"I had no idea taxes were going to be this much."

"I am so sick and tired of all my vendors calling me for payment!"

When you're in financial crisis mode, you're constantly being surprised by bad accounting news distracting you from what you really *need* to be doing to run and grow your business. You're simply not getting the information you need to run your business. Here's the catch: *you may not actually know what information you really need to run your business.* You just know you're not getting it.

I can always tell how long an entrepreneur has been in crisis mode by the black bags under their eyes. It's like reading the rings on a tree—many of them have been in crisis for *years.* While it's true that entrepreneurs are known for our resilience, we all have our breaking point. At that breaking point, crisis mode can go in one of two directions:

1. **Flaming out.** While some entrepreneurs simply wear down and call it quits, more often, someone quits on you—a lender, a key supplier, an employee, or anyone critical who hasn't gotten paid. However it happens, in some way the universe will intervene and say you're done. And when that happens, there's not much you

can do besides get back up, dust yourself off, and figure out what's next.

2. **Empowerment.** This means growing out of crisis mode and learning how to confidently direct your accounting team to get the information you need, when you need it, and in a format that works for you (simple, quick, and intuitive—not accountant-speak).

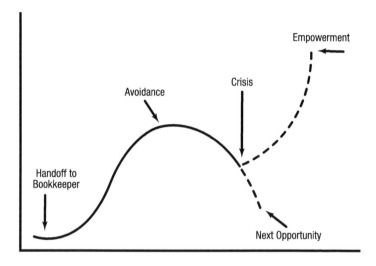

To be sure, you will face many challenges ahead (which we'll get to in just a moment). But first, here's what empowerment actually looks like:

- **Confidently direct your accounting team.** Know how to provide clear expectations and accountabilities to your accounting team (no more hiding in the corner hoping they do a good job).

- **Get the information you need.** Be confident about exactly what information you need to make good decisions for your business (no more unwanted surprises or lack of clarity).
- **When you need it.** Get information delivered to you on time on a regularly scheduled basis (no more having to remember to ask for various reports on an ad hoc basis when you have enough energy to review).
- **In a format that works for you.** This the *crux* of empowerment! Get your information in a format that is intuitive and easy to understand (no more accounting reports that you don't look at) and *quick* to review (no more long, painful reports!).
- **Have a plan of action for the biggest issues facing your business.** Confidently know how to take on your biggest financial challenges (no more shotgun approach to solving financial issues. Attack them with a laser beam.).

Naturally, you want to feel that way. I want you to have that kind of confidence too. To make it a reality, you first have to understand the three major factors standing between you and financial clarity.

THE THREE CRISIS FACTORS

There are three key reasons why entrepreneurs find themselves in crisis mode on a regular basis. I like to call these the F-Bombs, because every time you encounter one of them, you can't help but drop an F-bomb.

F-BOMB #1: SYSTEMS PROBLEMS

In the late 1990s, NASA invested over $125 million on the Mars Orbiter. It was designed to be the first weather station to orbit Mars. However, as it approached the planet, something went wrong, and the orbiter slipped into the atmosphere and was destroyed on entry.

This represented a catastrophic failure for NASA. Obviously, they launched an investigation. How did this 125-*million*-dollar project blow up in their faces? As it turned out, the software that powered the Orbiter's thrusters measured force in metric or newtons, whereas the software that picked up data and relayed it back to mission control measured in imperial or pounds. The two systems worked correctly, but the interface didn't calculate for the two different standards of measurement. This resulted in massive internal conflict; one system tried to pull the numbers up, while the other tried to pull the numbers down.

The result was an interplanetary F-bomb caused by a *very* avoidable problem!

In business terms, we often see the same kinds of systems failures. You, the entrepreneur, are out there exploring the universe in metric, while your accountants are back at mission control using imperial. You are literally speaking different languages using different systems. I (along with other designated accountants) went to school for years to learn how to set up, write, read, and interpret financial statements (i.e., understand the "imperial" system). You didn't. You also didn't go to entrepreneur school (most likely). Your schooling came from doing the job and you learned to speak and use "metric." Most accountants have never been entrepreneurs and didn't learn metric. They're stuck using imperial. How many failures have happened— or will happen—in your business because you and your accountant aren't speaking the common language of a shared system?

More importantly, imagine how much better things would be if you were confident you were using the same system and language. We'll look at making that happen starting in part 2 of the book.

F-BOMB #2: THE ACCOUNTING STACK AND PRICE OF ADMISSION

Taking the analogies back down to earth, imagine you're at a construction site. At the top of the "stack" of responsibility is the general contractor. Below that are the specialized trades or subtrades (carpenters, electricians, plumbers, etc.) handling a lot of technical work. At the bottom of the stack are the laborers doing the real grunt work on a construction site like digging ditches, hauling lumber, and sweeping up. It's an organized structure that makes intuitive sense and gets the job done right.

This same stack structure exits within your accounting department, but you might not intuitively recognize it as clearly as the construction example.

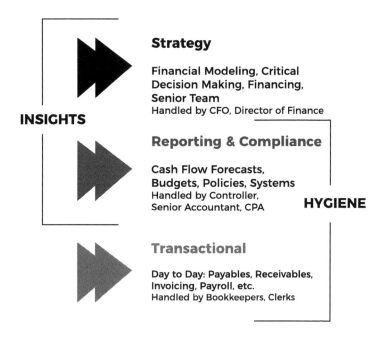

Transactional Function (Laborer Equivalent on a Job Site)

At the bottom of the stack are your bookkeepers or clerks. They handle the day-to-day transactions of the business, such as invoicing, payables, payroll, bank reconciliations, etc. (the grunt work of accounting). They are similar to the laborers on a construction site in that they generally don't have specialized training or schooling and anyone can call themselves a bookkeeper (or laborer).

Reporting and Compliance Function (Trades Equivalent on a Job Site)

Above the transactional function is the reporting and compliance function. As the name suggests, this includes your monthly reporting package—***including*** your cash flow forecasting and budgets (you do have budgets and cash flow forecasts, right? Right?). The compliance part of this function is often overlooked. Maybe because it's the boring of the boring part of an accounting department (even most accountants find this boring). This function includes a number of responsibilities:

- Setting up and updating your accounting P&Ps (processes and procedures, sometimes called SOPs— standard operating procedures), which outline how everything works in the accounting department.
- Selecting and implementing the right accounting software and apps for your needs.
- Creating and running your monthly reporting package.
- Setting up and updating the "chart of accounts" or "blueprints" of your financials.
- Overseeing the bookkeeper.

- Ensuring that your books are using accrual accounting, not cash accounting.

These people generally have job titles such as controller or assistant controller, among other names. You'll often see accountants with a CPA designation (although not all controllers are CPAs), as they have specialized skills.

Strategic Function (Contractor Equivalent on a Job Site)

On the top of the stack is the strategic function, which is handled by your CFO, VP of finance, or director of finance. They sit at the senior management table with you, and their job is to help you strategically look at your business through a financial lens. They may address questions such as these:

- What happens if we open another division or store?
- What happens if we change our pricing structure?
- Will we have enough cash five years from now based on the way we currently run our business?
- How are we going to get our hands on enough cash to implement our strategic initiatives over the next few years?

The strategic function also handles raising money either through conventional banks or through other means such as investors or subdebt lenders.

Combine these three tiers together, and you have your Accounting Stack. The problem is, most entrepreneurs don't even realize they *need* an Accounting Stack. And the F-bomb gets worse. Much worse.

The reality is, entrepreneurs who *most need* the full stack accounting help can *least afford it*. One look at Robert Half's 2019 Salary Guide median salary for the three key tiers of your Accounting Stack, and you'll see why:[6]

Strategy $101,500 - $497,250

Financial Modeling, Critical Decision Making, Financing, Senior Team
Handled by CFO, Director of Finance

INSIGHTS

$72,750 - $207,750

Reporting & Compliance

Cash Flow Forecasts, Budgets, Policies, Systems
Handled by Controller, Senior Accountant, CPA

HYGIENE

Transactional $28,250 - $65,750

Day to Day: Payables, Receivables, Invoicing, Payroll, etc.
Handled by Bookkeepers, Clerks

---

6   See https://www.roberthalf.com/salary-guide/accounting-and-finance. Note: This link may change from time to time. You can simply Google "Robert Half Salary Guide," and you'll be able to find the most current version. It comes out every year. There is also a table in there that will allow you to index the costs of each role to your home city.

The cost to staff the entire Accounting Stack is at least a couple hundred thousand dollars. And that's at the *low end*. Guess what type of accountants you're getting if you're always hiring at the low end?

Let that F-bomb sink in for a moment.

If you're doing $2 million to $3 million (or even $5 million to $10 million) or less in revenue, you likely aren't able to absorb that kind of expense; your entire accounting department is most likely just a bookkeeper. So, you toss everything at your bookkeeper and expect them to handle **all** of your needs *throughout the Accounting Stack*. Guess what?

That would be the *exact* same as hiring a laborer to handle every aspect of building you a house.

They are *part* of the solution, but you'd never expect them to handle the entire job. That's not what they were trained to do. They can't do everything, and you need to stop expecting them to!

Hygiene vs. Insights

Looking back at the Accounting Stack above, the other item of note is the "Hygiene" line capturing the bottom half of the stack and the "Insights" line capturing the top half. We'll get into more detail about both Hygiene and Insights later in on the book, but here's what I'll say for now: The Hygiene is really all of the stuff you likely think of as accounting—all of the day-to-day transactions, your monthly financials, etc.

But here's the thing. The Hygiene is NOT for you! It's for accountants like me and the bankers we send it to.

What is for you is the Insights. This is the information that actually helps you make the right decisions for your business. There's a good chance that if you're in crisis mode, it's because not only is your team struggling to deliver good, quality Hygiene, but they're also struggling to deliver Insights. So, you can't make good decisions for your business. This F-bomb cuts deep!

TO ENTREPRENEURS

Throughout this book, I'll be talking about both external and internal accountants (mostly internal). Sometimes it can be difficult to distinguish between the two groups because, well, both refer to themselves as accountants. It's important that we make that distinction now.

The members of your Accounting Stack are your internal accountant(s), whether you outsource those positions or not and as mentioned above are a mix of CPAs and non-CPAs.

Outside of your Accounting Stack are your external accountants. These are trained CPAs who work in public accounting firms, such as Ernst & Young or Deloitte (etc.), although many work either independently or in a countless number of smaller and medium-size accounting firms.

External accountants can do a lot of different things for you. Most entrepreneurs think of them as handling "year-ends" and filing taxes. Year-ends are typically called a "Notice to Reader" or "Review Engagement." "Audits" are also a type of year-end, typically done for much larger or public companies. External CPAs also do corporate and personal taxes, as well as business and IT consulting, mergers and acquisitions, valuations, and other specialty services not handled by your internal accounting team.

Most likely, you're accustomed to having both your internal Accounting Stack (or maybe just "Peggy," your bookkeeper) and your external accountant. A lot of entrepreneurs are expecting business advice from their external accountants. Sometimes, you'll get great advice. Sometimes, you won't. Just like the rest of the people in the Accounting Stack, your external accountant likely has a specific area of expertise (like preparing a year-end). They may not be a business analyst (or even business generalist), and providing advice may not be in their wheelhouse. A lot of entrepreneurs express frustration at their year-end accountant not giving them good advice. Like your Accounting Stack, are you expecting your external accountant to have skills they weren't trained in? Is that why you're frustrated?

F-BOMB #3: THE MENTAL/EMOTIONAL PROBLEM

Once, after giving a talk to a group of entrepreneurs, I was mingling with the guests—a mixed crowd of both entrepreneurs and their accountants. One woman, a bookkeeper, approached me, and almost immediately she was in tears.

"No matter what I say, my boss doesn't seem to get it. He never hears me," she said. "He keeps starting all these new initiatives, but *we don't have the money for all this stuff and he just won't stop!*"

I haven't seen or talked to this bookkeeper since, especially because she broke off our conversation and literally ran out of the room crying (uh, not because of our conversation... just to be clear.). Shortly after the presentation I was invited to lunch with the very entrepreneur who had her in tears. His mood after my talk was markedly different. In a word, he was "stoked." "I can't wait to start implementing some of this stuff!"

To me, this perfectly sums up our third F-bomb: It's not just that the bookkeeper and the entrepreneur speak different languages; it's that they see the exact same issue from completely different viewpoints! The entrepreneur sees opportunity where problems are bumps in the road to be figured out along the way. Don't have enough money for a new initiative? No problem! We'll figure it out later.

The accountant, however, often gets hyperfocused seeing the problems that need to be addressed. They are risk-averse to a fault. Business problems become compounded because entrepreneurs and accountants look at life through such different lenses. The accountant is focused on things that entrepreneurs aren't worried about, and the entrepreneurs aren't getting what they need because the accountants can't see their vision.

The result: you run over your bookkeeper, and they end up keeping their mouth shut until they run out of the room crying.

Add that to F bomb #1 (you're using different languages) and F bomb #2 (you're expecting things from your book-keeper they were never trained to do), and you can easily see how you ended up in crisis mode, unable to get the numbers you need to run your business.

EXERCISE: FROM F-BOMBS TO EMPOWERMENT

Now that you know the three F-bombs and understand why you might be in accounting pain, here's an exercise to help you better understand what empowerment feels like.

Take a moment and think about the biggest financial issue facing your business today, and what it's costing you in terms of profit or cash. To be clear, I'm not talking about issues like "I don't have any money in my bank account" or "We're not profitable." Those are results. Instead, focus on the cause. For example:

The issue: My labor costs me 3 percent more than it should.

The cost: $120,000 a year.

Or:

The issue: My overhead costs have gone up 4.5 percent faster than sales have.

The cost: $87,000 in profit a year.

Now it's your turn: Write down the single biggest issue facing your business. Next, write down your second biggest and third-biggest issues. Now, rank order them in terms of impact on cash and/or impact on profit.

Be honest: Are you truly clear on the Top 3 financial issues facing your business? Do you know precisely what they're costing you each month, or each year? Do you have that level of insight into your business?

The empowered entrepreneur has absolute clarity and certainty over the top issues facing their business. If you don't, what issues are you spending your time addressing? Are you going after the biggest issues, or are you spinning your wheels fixing problems that are relatively insignificant?

When I ask this question among groups of entrepreneurs, I

usually get blank stares or looks of "intense thought" (read: I don't know, but I want to look like I do). The truth is, most of us don't know the biggest problems facing our business. We certainly know we *have* problems, but we don't know what to focus on first, second, and third. We lack the insight to act—and therefore we **lack empowerment**.

Whatever problems you might be facing can be measured and quantified. Your financial statements are *dying* to tell you a story. They're *dying* to tell you all the biggest issues facing your business. The rest of this book will teach you how to direct your accounting team to get the right information, at the right time, and in a form that works for you. When you can unearth those stories, you'll be surprised how quickly you move from spewing F-bombs to celebrating empowerment.

TO BOOKKEEPERS

If your job is purely transactional, be careful. In the chapters ahead, I'm going to be telling your boss exactly how the world is changing—and why you might not have a job in a few years. It's time to step up your skillset to become at least a "tradesperson"—if not a general contractor—if you want to keep bringing home those paychecks.

CHAPTER 2

THE FEELING OF EMPOWERMENT

On a scale of one to ten, how empowered do you feel when it comes to your numbers? How clearly do you understand the financial position of your business? Are you clear on the key financial issues facing your business? Do you have a plan of action for dealing with those key issues?

To help you rate yourself, here is a questionnaire:

QUESTION	YES	NO	KINDA
1. I clearly understand my current financial position.			
2. I clearly understand the Top 3 issues facing my business through a financial lens.			
3. I understand what's not a major financial issue and can therefore clear the mental clutter from my brain.			
4. I have a plan of action dealing with those Top 3 issues.			
5. My financial information is delivered to me in a simple-to-understand, intuitive way.			
6. I am clear on what a great reporting package looks like.			
7. I can confidently direct my accounting team to get the financial information I need in a format that works for me.			
8. My financial information arrives to me at the same time each month in the same format (unless agreed-upon changes are being made).			
9. I can complete my monthly financial review quickly (in less than 15 minutes per month).			
10. I can complete my financial review outlined in #1–#9 above without having to look at an actual set of financial statements.			

Here's how to score yourself: 1 point for yes, ½ point for kinda, and 0 points for no. Total it up, and that's your empowerment scale.

How did you do?

Usually when I give this questionnaire to a room full of entrepreneurs, the numbers come back fairly low. Occasionally, someone will rate themselves a seven or an eight—I've never seen a perfect ten. For most entrepreneurs, their empowerment level is around three or four. So, if you scored low, you're not alone.

Such low numbers are far from ideal, and yet they're the norm! The question is, what can we do to feel more empowered? How do we turn those threes and fours into the eights, nines, and tens we all want them to be? That's exactly what this chapter is about.

GETTING TO EMPOWERMENT

The exercises in this chapter are designed to give you a taste of empowerment by giving you a sense of what life will look like *after* you implement the rest of the recommendations in this book. "Begin with the end in mind," as Steven Covey would say.

Before we begin, let's be real about a couple of things.

First, take a moment to skim ahead through the next few pages. Did you feel a little nervous seeing all those charts and graphs scattered throughout the following exercises? Didn't I say this wasn't an accounting lesson? What gives?

Trust me, it's not an accounting lesson—and it's not as bad as you think. All I'm asking you to do is look at a few charts, get a basic understanding about the good trends and the bad ones, and make a few high-level decisions. That's your job here, and that's your job for the business. Put in just a little bit of work here, and you'll be able to coast through these reports every month in less time and with more clarity than you ever have before.

This brings me to my second point: I'm guessing you're not going to actually do these exercises. How do I know? Because I'm an entrepreneur-type just like you, and I *never* do the exercises in books like this. But maybe you'll surprise me.

The point here is empowerment and for you to understand how this process works. To that end, I've done the exercises for you and suggested answers to the questions. If you disagree with my answers, no problem. That means you're paying attention. That's great—you'll get a better sense of things if you go through the steps and answer them in the context of your own business anyway. In any case, the real hands-on work (and by this I mean the work you'll be asking your Accounting Stack to perform) will come later in the book.

TO ACCOUNTANTS

The following exercises are an example of how you should be sharing information with your entrepreneur. Your entrepreneur doesn't understand the confusing spreadsheets and abstract terms in the giant binder of financials you usually give them. Keep reading to see how it's done.

EXERCISE 1: YOUR NEW MONTHLY REVIEW (A CASE STUDY)

You are the owner of Upside-Down Creative, a (fictitious) full-service digital agency. You do about $2 million a year in revenue. It's the middle of February, and it's time to sit down with your bookkeeper or controller (whoever is the most senior person in your Accounting Stack) and review your numbers.[7] Instead of looking through your numbers as you always have, your accountant leads you through the following monthly review.

What you should realize as you move through this presentation is that you need to know nothing about the details to understand what these charts are telling you. All you have to do is follow the lines on the graph to realize whether you're in good shape or you're in trouble.

CASH FLOW

Beginning with your cash flow forecast, take a look at the following chart. What do you notice about your future cash flow?

---

7   Two things to note: (1) All this data, though used here in context of a fictional business, is largely based on data from a real company. Real businesses face these exact issues every day. (2) Upside-Down Creative is a service-based business. If you are in manufacturing or otherwise have inventory, you will need some additional analysis, which we will scatter throughout this book.

Cash Flow Forecast

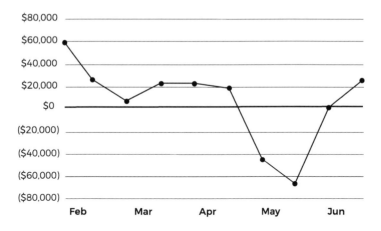

No doubt, you've noticed a big dip in your cash flow. Dig in a bit deeper and answer the following questions:

QUESTION	YOUR ANSWER	SUGGESTED ANSWER (IF YOU'RE NOT ACTUALLY GOING TO DO THE EXERCISES)
Is Cash Flow going the right way or wrong way?		Wrong way
Are you going to run into a cash problem at any point?		Yes
If yes, when?		Mid/late May–about three or four months from now.
If yes, how big an issue is this going to be?		About a $70K issue
Any other items of note?		There is a recovery toward the end. This looks like a short-term problem.
Is this something you feel like you would like to dig into a bit more? Does it require more work?		Yes

Right about now, you're almost certainly unhappy with your future cash flow. I get it. Make a note and continue through everything else, and then we'll get into what to do about it.

NET INCOME (A.K.A. NET PROFIT)

The next chart is looking at your net income each month this year. The dotted line is this year, the gray line is last year, and the black line is your budget for the year. Let's look *only* at this month (January) to answer these questions:

Net Income - Month

QUESTION	YOUR ANSWER	SUGGESTED ANSWER (IF YOU'RE NOT ACTUALLY GOING TO DO THE EXERCISES)
Is this year (dotted line) above or below last year (gray line)?		Above
Is this year (dotted line) above or below budget (black line)?		Above
Would you say your net income is on track for this month, or does it look like there is a problem?		Given net income is above our budget and last year, so I'd say things are on track for this month.

Look at the same net income information aggregated for the year (year-to-date, or YTD). With the line colors meaning the same thing (dotted is this year, gray is last year, and black is budget), answer the following questions:

Net Income - Year to Date

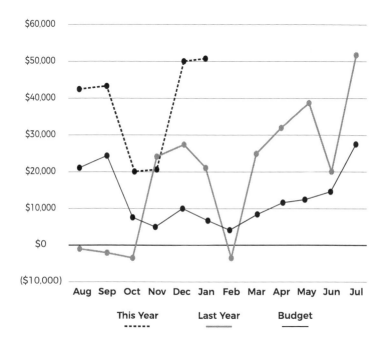

QUESTION	YOUR ANSWER	SUGGESTED ANSWER (IF YOU'RE NOT ACTUALLY GOING TO DO THE EXERCISES)
Is this year (dotted line) above or below last year (gray line)?		Above
Is this year (dotted line) above or below budget (black line)?		Above
Would you say your net income is on track this year to date (YTD), or does it look like there is a problem?		Given net income is above our budget and last year, so I'd say things are on track for this year.
Does the trend look to be on track, or is it heading the wrong direction?		On track
Do you feel like your net income is something you would like to dig into a bit more? Does it require more work?		No, it looks to be on track and actually better than budget.

So, you've noticed that your net income is better than budget, better than last year, and trending the right way. For now, we don't have to worry about it. On to the next section.

SALES

Next is sales. Notice we started with cash flow, then profit, and only then, sales. A lot of us start with sales because it makes us feel good because it's usually a nice big number (a.k.a. a "feel-good metric"). In reality, we should be starting with cash and then profit because that's what you really need to pay the bill and give yourself a nice dividend.

For sales, the process is exactly the same. Look at both the monthly and YTD charts, and then answer the simple questions:

Sales - Month

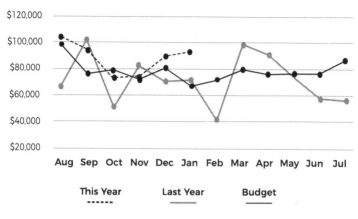

Sales - Year to Date

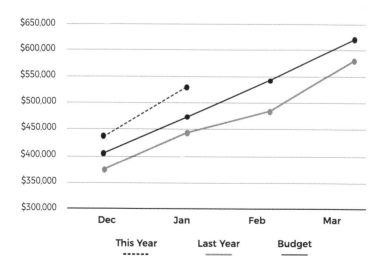

QUESTION	YOUR ANSWER	SUGGESTED ANSWER (IF YOU'RE NOT ACTUALLY GOING TO DO THE EXERCISES)
Is this year (dotted line) above or below last year (gray line)?		Above
Is this year (dotted line) above or below budget (black line)?		Above
Would you say your sales is on track for this month, or does it look like there is a problem?		Given sales is above our budget and last year, so I'd say things are on track for this month.
Does the trend look to be on track, or is it heading the wrong direction?		On track
Do you feel like sales is something you would like to dig into a bit more? Does it require more work?		No

TO ENTREPRENEURS

By now, you've realized there's not much to this process. This is the conversation that you *should* be having with your accountant. One by one, they walk you through the same thing with each critical piece of information in your business. If you can compare this year and last year against your budget and know if you're tending better or worse, then you can start to make decisions that will help your business.

If for some reason this *isn't* super intuitive or obvious to you just yet, I suggest you start again. You'll get it. Otherwise, keep reading so you can see how we keep applying this process to other aspects of your business.

GROSS MARGIN (A.K.A. GROSS CONTRIBUTION)

Next, on to gross margin—the one accounting term we can't really get away from because it's critical. According to Investopedia, "Gross profit margin measures the amount of revenue that remains after subtracting costs directly associated with production."

For an agency like Upside-Down Creative, the formula would be: revenue – direct labor costs (web developers, writers, editors, contractors, etc.), production costs (camera rentals, printing costs, etc.), and other costs directly related to completing the job, but *before* any overhead costs. That leaves you with gross margin. Which you want to see as *high* as possible to make as much money on your jobs as possible.

Again, look at the monthly and YTD charts and answer a few simple questions:

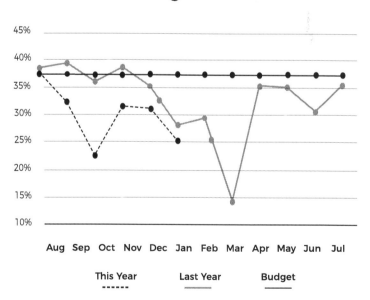

Gross Margin - Month

This Year   Last Year   Budget

Gross Margin - Year

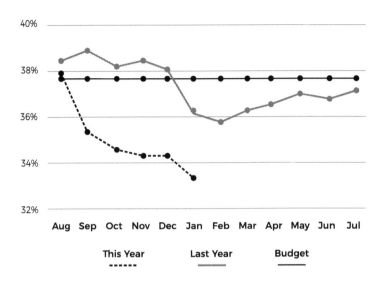

QUESTION	YOUR ANSWER	SUGGESTED ANSWER (IF YOU'RE NOT ACTUALLY GOING TO DO THE EXERCISES)
Is this year (dotted line) above or below last year (gray line)?		Below
Is this year (dotted line) above or below budget (black line)?		Below
Would you say your gross margin is on track for this month, or does it look like there is a problem?		Given gross margin is below our budget and last year, so I'd say things are definitely *off track*.
Does the trend look to be on track, or is it heading the wrong direction?		Off track
Do you feel like gross margin is something you would like to dig into a bit more? Does it require more work?		*Yes!*

Add this to your list of items you want to dig deeper into after the initial review. So far, you should have cash forecast and gross margin on your list.

OVERHEAD COSTS

You might also see these called "SG&A" or "Sales, General, and Admin" costs. These are the costs not included in your gross margin—in other words, the day-to-day costs of running the business, such as office rent, phones, and admin labor (like reception and accountants). Overhead is anything that supports running the business, but isn't directly related to delivering your product or service.

Have a look at the following charts and then answer those same questions:

Overhead Expenses - Month

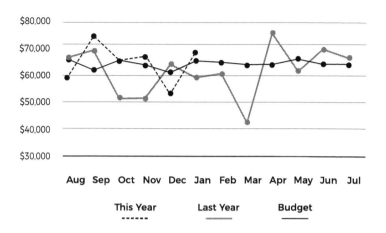

	This Year	Last Year	Budget

Overhead Expenses - Year to Date

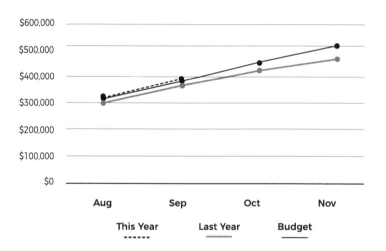

	This Year	Last Year	Budget

QUESTION	YOUR ANSWER	SUGGESTED ANSWER (IF YOU'RE NOT ACTUALLY GOING TO DO THE EXERCISES)
Is this year (dotted line) above or below last year (gray line)?		A little above the month A little above year to date
Is this year (dotted line) above or below budget (black line)?		Very close
Would you say your overhead expenses are on track for this month, or does it look like there is a problem?		Given overhead expenses are pretty close to our plan (budget) for the year, I'd say it's OK, but will have to keep an eye on it going forward.
Does the trend look to be on track, or is it heading the wrong direction?		On track
Do you feel like overhead expenses is something you would like to dig into a bit more? Does it require more work?		It's close, but since the year to date is pretty on budget, I'd say we can set it aside for now, but keep a close eye on it going forward.

ACCOUNTS RECEIVABLE (AR)

Looking at the following AR charts, what do you notice? For clarity, we are looking at your AR in two ways.

1. Total Days Your AR Is Outstanding

This line chart is showing your "days outstanding" AR for this year and last year. If the number is fifty-six, it means it takes you on average fifty-six days to get paid. If the number is twenty-two, then it's twenty-two days. Obviously, the lower the number the better.

Accounts Receivables - Days

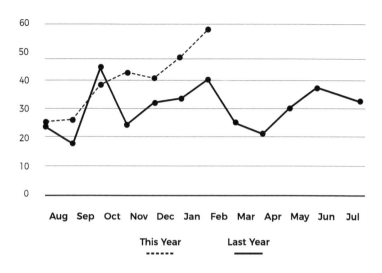

This Year
- - - - - -

Last Year
───────

2. Amount Outstanding by Aging "Bucket"

This shows your AR based on how many days *overdue* your receivable is. If it's current, then it's not yet due. If it shows up in the thirty- to sixty-day bucket, then it's saying your client is late paying between one and two months! This data is represented by the pie chart.

Accounts Receivables - Aging

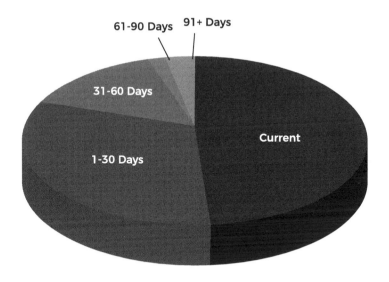

QUESTION	YOUR ANSWER	SUGGESTED ANSWER (IF YOU'RE NOT ACTUALLY GOING TO DO THE EXERCISES)
Are your AR days on the line chart higher or lower than last year?		Higher
Is the trend of the line chart getting better (going down) or getting worse (going up)?		Getting worse
Looking at the pie, are you happy or unhappy with how much of your accounts are overdue?		Very unhappy. It's showing over 1/2 of our AR is overdue!
Do you feel like AR collections is something you would like to dig into a bit more? Does it require more work?		Yes, definitely!

ACCOUNTS PAYABLE (AP)

This is a quick look to make sure nothing looks wrong here. Looking at the following AP pie chart, what do you notice? (Note, this works the same as your AR pie chart, showing how many days *overdue* your payable is by aging bucket. If it's current, then it's not yet due.

Accounts Payables - Aging

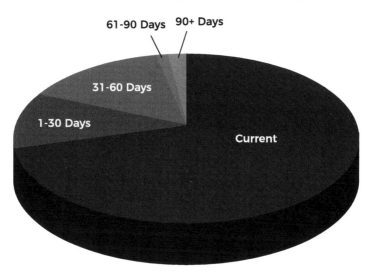

QUESTION	YOUR ANSWER	SUGGESTED ANSWER (IF YOU'RE NOT ACTUALLY GOING TO DO THE EXERCISES)
Looking at the pie, are you happy or unhappy with how much of your accounts are overdue?		Looks OK. There are a couple of older-looking payables I'll look into, but it seems OK for now.
Do you feel like AR collections is something you would like to dig into a bit more? Does it require more work?		No

WHERE TO PROBE?

Look back over the past few exercises. For which charts did you answer that the area requires more work? Write them into the following table. If you're still not sure, don't worry. I've taken the liberty of filling in some suggested answers.

ISSUES NOTED FOR DEEPER DIVE

	YOUR ISSUES FOR DEEPER DIVE	SUGGESTED ANSWERS
ISSUE 1		Cash flow forecast
ISSUE 2		Gross margin
ISSUE 3		Accounts receivable
ISSUE 4		
ISSUE 5		

Here's what you should know at this point: You're unhappy with your cash flow, you're unhappy with your gross margin, you're unhappy about accounts receivable, and you're keeping an eye on overhead expenses. The silver lining? Everything else appears to be in either good or decent shape. While you don't know everything about your books, you now have a clear picture of the important high-level financial measures of your business.[8] You know whether you're happy or unhappy, and whether you need to follow up on any particular issues inside your business.

---

8   Remember, this is a sample company and your charts will almost certainly need to be tweaked to suit your business. Don't assume these charts are exactly what you need. They are a great place to start, but we'll be going into more detail in parts 3 and 4 of the book.

That alone might give you more clarity about the state of your business than you've ever had before, and it can be done in less than three minutes once you've been through it a couple of times and are comfortable with reading the charts without going back to the text.

With that, now is a perfect time to check in. Remember your empowerment score from the beginning of the chapter? What is it now? If you had this set of charts for your business every month and you spent three minutes reviewing it, how empowered would you feel? Has it grown to a five, a six, or even a seven? Are you starting to feel more empowered?

If not, try charting these numbers out for your own business, or keep reading ahead and see if something clicks. If that magical feeling of empowerment still doesn't come, head to Entreprenumbers.com for some extra resources to help you get over the top. Maybe watching a video of this will help it click.

EXECUTIVE SUMMARY OF EXERCISE 1

Through this exercise, you've discovered what you are happy with, or unhappy with, in your business in three minutes or less. Empowerment starts with financial clarity.

EXERCISE 2: THE TOP THREE FINANCIAL ISSUES FACING YOUR BUSINESS

In this exercise, you will begin to understand the Top 3 issues facing your business (in this case, Upside Down Creative). When your Accounting Stack is firing on all cylinders, understanding the Top 3 issues facing your business should be as simple as looking at this chart:

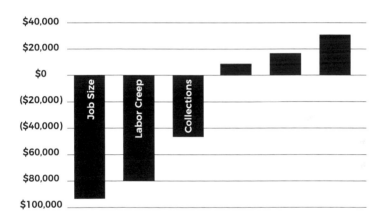

Top 3 Insights

Don't worry, your job is not to create this chart. That's your accountant's job, just like it's also their job to explain it to you in a way that you understand and answer any questions you have. Your accountant will provide that explanation in a moment. However, before they do, you should already be able to clearly see the Top 3 issues facing your business and how big the issues are rank ordered by impact on cash or impact on profit.

ISSUE 1: JOB SIZE

In our last year at Upside-Down Creative, we worked ninety-seven individual jobs. We took those ninety-seven jobs and split them into big jobs (above $10,000 revenue) and small jobs (below $10,000 revenue).

We found that fifty-seven of those ninety-seven jobs were small jobs, while only forty were big jobs. Here's the catch: those fifty-seven small jobs only account for 8 (*eight!*) percent of your revenue. Yes, almost 60 percent of your jobs represented *only* 8 percent of your revenue.

Jobs

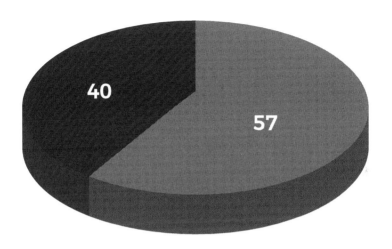

 Jobs Under $10k  Jobs Over $10k

Revenue

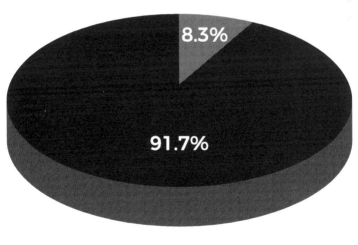

Jobs Under $10k  Jobs Over $10k

Or course, regardless of the size of each job we took at Upside-Down Creative, we had to scope it, quote it, win it, staff it, manage it, deliver it, invoice it, collect it, and make sure everything went smoothly. Ask yourself, who are your problem clients, the ones that complain the most? Are they the big clients or the small ones? Most likely the small ones, and you find yourself super annoyed running around solving problems for your smallest clients all the time. So over and above everything you already have to do for them, you also have to troubleshoot them and give them extra attention.

Because of how much staff time and effort goes into each of those small jobs, we calculated that each of those jobs is actually *losing* an average of $1,500 per job. With almost sixty small jobs, that's costing around $90,000 per year!

This is our single biggest financial issue! Too many jobs, and more specifically, too many small jobs. You have likely already started solving this issue in your mind. Eliminate a bunch of the fifty-seven small jobs, keep the strategic ones, raise our minimums, etc. That's great—solving problems is what entrepreneurs do best. But before you do, it's important to finish the Top 3 analysis first.

Ask yourself this: When you hear that almost 60 percent of your jobs only accounted for 8 percent of your revenue, does it make intuitive sense that they are costing you more money than you are making? If you're struggling with this one, ask some experienced entrepreneur friends of yours what they think.

Go ahead and add it to the "Issues Noted for Deeper Dive" list you made at the end of Exercise 1.

> ## TO ACCOUNTANTS
>
> If you're thinking it would be better to measure contribution per job, you're absolutely right! If you have job costing set up properly, go for it. Revenue is an easier concept for some, which is why it is used here. But contribution per job would be an even better analysis than revenue per job. Just be sure it is clear and easy to understand.

ISSUE 2: LABOR CREEP

Labor creep has nothing to do with the sketchiness of your hires. That's a matter for HR, not accounting. In accounting-speak, "labor creep" has to do with your cost of labor, which at Upside-Down has grown by 3.8 percent in the last two years. In other words, for every dollar of revenue you sell today, you earn 3.8 percent less than you did two years ago because your labor costs 3.8 percent more to produce the same value of jobs. Clearly, that's not good.

Labor Creep

3.8%

The math is pretty simple. When you're bringing in roughly $2 million in revenue with nearly 4 percent increase (as a percentage of sales) in labor costs, you're losing around $80,000 in profitability. Look back at the list on at the end of exercise 1. Remember how you added gross margin as an issue you wanted to dig into later? It turns out that the root issue was labor.

Does this also make intuitive sense? Is it clear to you that this is a problem? If yes, go to your issues list and scratch out "gross margin" and replace it with "labor."

ISSUE 3: ACCOUNTS RECEIVABLE

You already called this out as an issue in the first exercise. Let's dig in a bit deeper. Last year, it took between twenty and forty days after the due date to collect your money. Call it thirty days on average. Now, it's taking fifty-seven days—

almost *twice* as long. It's taking almost a month longer to collect from your clients than it did last year.

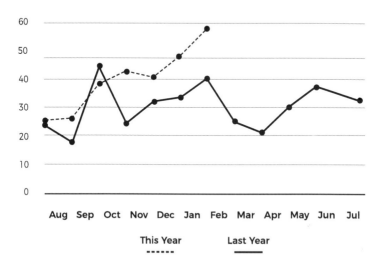

Accounts Receivables - Days

So what? Think about everything you're paying for—your employees, your rent, your phone bills, and your computer bills. Now, think about all the money you *haven't received* in the last fifty-seven days. Had you been collecting your accounts receivable at the thirty-day mark like you were averaging last year, you would have an extra $45,000 in your jeans. But you don't. Instead, all that money is sitting in your client's bank account and you're operating without it.

Since you've already added it to the list at the end of exercise 1, there's nothing more to do but gain confidence in understanding what your key issues are.

KNOWLEDGE IS POWER

At this point, you have your top issues identified and rank ordered by impact on your business. While the actual dollar amount of the cash flow forecast issue isn't the largest of the issues, it gets moved to the top of the list because you obviously can't survive without solving this issue. Cash always comes first.

ISSUE	IMPACT	NOTE
Cash flow forecast	$70,000 cash shortfall	From exercise 1.
		We will run out of cash in 3–4 months and be up to $70K underwater.
Job size	$90,000 profit impact	From exercise 2
		Roughly 60 percent of our jobs are generating only 8 percent of our revenue.
Labor creep (the gross margin problem from exercise 1)	$80,000 profit impact	From exercise 1 and 2
		Our labor costs have grown by almost 4 percent compared to labor cost in the prior years, which is dragging our gross margin down.
Accounts receivable days	$45,000 cash impact	From exercise 1 and 2
		We are collecting slow by almost a full month.

How are you feeling now? How clear would you be if you had a rank-ordered list of the key issues facing your business delivered to you every month? No guessing. No analysis. Just a simple chart for you to take and build a plan.

At this point, you might be wondering about all the other issues facing your business. There aren't just four!

Are you just supposed to ignore them?

Yes—but only for now. For argument's sake, let's pretend meals and entertainment, your seventh most important issue, is $6,000 over budget and $5,200 over where it was last year. No one likes shelling out an extra six grand when they don't have to, but I'd rather spend my time dealing with $90K, $80K, $70K, and $45K issues first. Sure, if the $6,000 problem is an easy fix, go for it.

Just don't lose sight of the big picture. It's easy to get caught up caught in all the small issues facing your business without tackling the big ones. However, it's the big issues that are going to make or break your business. Don't worry, you can squeeze the lemon on meals and entertainment (no pun intended) when you've got the big issues under control. In the meantime, you get to eliminate the mental noise caused by all of these small issues and not worry about them until the bigger issues are solved.

Once the process is up and running, understanding your Top 3 shouldn't take more than a few minutes per month, and your total monthly package review shouldn't be more than five minutes for charts and Top 3.[9]

---

9   You may be wondering why we have 4 issues in our Top 3 exercise. Good catch! Call me a liar with a Top 3. The idea is it's the top *few* issues facing the business. If there are 2, fine. If you have 4 or 5, that's OK too. The point is you keep the list short so you can solve the biggest issues of the business with laser focus and don't get distracted on the non-issues.

Having completed exercise 2, how empowered are you feeling now on a scale of one to ten? Remind yourself where you started and where you were after exercise 1. Did you move the needle even more after exercise 2? If not and you prefer to see this in video format, head to Entrepnumbers.com to watch the case study rather than read it. It might make things click if you're feeling stuck.

EXECUTIVE SUMMARY OF EXERCISE 2

Through this exercise, you gained valuable insights into your business and now know where to focus your energy.

When you can identify your Top 3 issues, then you have clarity of purpose. You're empowered to act. The "Insights Analysis" section of the reporting package in part 3 is a step-by-step approach to direct your accounting team on how to identify your Top 3 issues across four broad categories.

EXERCISE 3: BRAINSTORMING TO SOLVE THE ISSUES

Now that you know the top issues facing your business, it's time to work out a plan. Whatever issue you are facing, someone has solved it before. Rather than trying to sort it out on your own, lean on others—mastermind groups, mentors, biz school teachers, entrepreneur friends, or even Dr. Google. Just don't lean on your accountants![10]

For each of the key issues, write down the top strategies you

---

10   Accountants, I'm kidding. It would be awesome if you showed up with some ideas when you present the issues. In fact, entrepreneurs are expecting it!

will execute to resolve the problem. Note that sometimes the strategy is getting more information. The point of these charts and the Top 3 issues list is to put you in a position to ask more questions and dig deeper where needed.

ISSUE	YOUR SOLUTION	SUGGESTED SOLUTIONS[11]
Cash shortfall in 3-4 months growing to $70K		Collect overdue receivables ($45K). Get a line of credit from the bank. Change customer payment terms to 50 percent down for all new orders. Hold vendor payments by a week or two.
Number of small jobs is costing us almost $90K in profitability.		Set a minimum revenue per job and do not accept any new jobs below the threshold unless strategic reason. Raise prices on all "small" jobs and make sure they are truly profitable (ensure costing of each job is complete and reviewed by accounting). Dig in a bit deeper and see which specific jobs are the problem. Is it a type of service offering? Type of client? Change marketing strategy to target larger jobs (longer-term solution).
Labor grew almost 4 percent more than sales, costing us almost $80K in profitability		Hiring freeze until labor gets back in line. Terminate the lowest performers (there are no hard decisions in business, just sad ones). Review process flow for inefficiencies and waste (lean concepts).

ISSUE	YOUR SOLUTION	SUGGESTED SOLUTIONS[11]
AR is nearly two months overdue and we have $45K less in the bank because of it.		Pick up the phone and call the overdue accounts.
		Freeze work on all jobs until accounts are collected ("encourage" clients to pay on time).
		Change payment terms to deposit and/or milestone payments for all future jobs.

Again, it's time to check in on your empowerment scale. You now know your current financial positions, the key financial issues facing your business, the nonissues that you can let go of, and you now have a plan of action to deal with those issues (not to mention that we never even looked at a set of financial statements!). If you were able to receive this information every month and brainstorm solutions—often in as little as fifteen minutes per month—how empowered would you feel on a scale of one to ten? How much have you shifted?

EXECUTIVE SUMMARY OF EXERCISE 3

Albert Einstein is reported to have once said, "If I had an hour to solve a problem, I'd spend fifty-five minutes thinking about the problem and five minutes thinking about solutions."[12] The good news is your accountant did a lot of the fifty-five minutes worth of heavy lifting. It's your job to solve the big issues. Get out of the details and focus on the most important issues. Do that and your business will look a lot different as you continue to knock off the biggest issues first!

---

11 This is not a comprehensive list. These are just examples of what can be done with these issues we've uncovered.

12 According to Google, there's some debate as to whether Einstein actually said this. I'd always heard it attributed to him, but I could be wrong. No matter who said it, it's a genius quote.

Now that you know how to understand and act on your financials in just fifteen minutes a month, you should be well on the road to being the fully empowered entrepreneur you deserve to be. The fully empowered entrepreneur has six key elements:

1. **You clearly understand your current financial position.** At any time, you have a clear picture of where you stand compared to your plan (i.e., budget) and the last year. Are you trending the right way or the wrong way?

2. **You know, with confidence, the Top 3 financial issues facing your business, so you can focus your energy and attention on them.** If you don't know the top issues, you might be trying to fix every issue (or worse, small irrelevant issues). You can't. Focus on the biggest issues. That's going to have the biggest impact.

3. **Your mind is clear of everything that isn't a Top 3 issue.** The problem with *not* being empowered is you worry about everything. Empowerment is also about giving yourself some mental relief. As you focus on your Top 3 issues, shove all other financial concerns to the back of your mind.

4. **Effectively brainstorm solutions to your biggest problem.** Leveraging a peer network,[13] mastermind group, mentors or even Google, quickly get to a plan of

---

13   I highly recommend the Entrepreneurs' Organization, which I've been an active member of since 2005.

action for your Top 3 issues. You're not the first person with these issues, so take a shortcut to get to the plan.

5. **Done in fifteen minutes or less per month.** Sometimes the brainstorming might take a little longer, but within fifteen minutes, you should *always* be able to understand your financial position, including the Top 3 issues you must tackle and get a jump on a path to solutions.

6. **You can do all of these without ever opening your actual financial statements.** This is the best part. When the information is delivered to you in a format *you* understand, you can do away with traditional financial statements and introduce intuitive, understandable, and actionable reports that you will come to know and love (yes, I said "love" when referring to month-end review).

Where are you on the empowerment scale now? An eight, a nine, maybe even a ten? When you have this kind of insight, you have power. If not, run through the exercise again or visit Entreprenumbers.com. You'll get there once you get familiar with the format.

You don't need to become an accountant to understand your numbers. You just need to know how to confidently direct your accounting team to get the information you need when you need it and in a format that works for you. Now you have a taste of what that looks like. In parts 2 and

3 of the book, I will walk you through the exact steps you need to direct your team to make this approach a reality.

TO THE ACCOUNTANT

Did you catch all that? It sounds pretty plain, like anyone could understand it, right? Before moving on, take a look again at the six steps to financial empowerment. Now ask yourself, how can you provide this level of clarity to your entrepreneur without confusing them? How can you provide the information they need to know without ever showing them any financial statements?

If you're a bookkeeper, you likely need to upgrade your analytics skills. Learn how to do the types of analysis I mentioned, and learn how to present them in intuitive chart forms.

Remember, the game is changing on you–both in terms of technological advancements and expectations. Don't get left in the dust!

PART 2

LEVERS

You've probably heard the quote "Give me a lever long enough and a fulcrum on which to place it, and I shall move the world." While I'm not prone to quoting Archimedes, the point of this quote is massively relevant to our topic. Specifically, a huge element of empowerment is understanding the *key levers* of your business which drive increased cash flow and/or increased profitability. Looking at the six elements of empowerment from the last chapter, the first point is understanding your current financial position. Diving a bit deeper into that, it's actually understanding your current financial position *and* the key levers of your business.

There are actually only a *few* key levers that you can pull on to impact profit and/or cash flow in your business, and they are baked into the charts section of your monthly report. In fact, you've probably seen them a million times, but you may not have realized they are indeed the levers.

Building a package that is intuitive to understand and that focuses on the key levers *and* the biggest issues would make Archimedes proud, and allow you to lean on the parts of the business that will have the biggest positive impact.

CHAPTER 3

IDENTIFYING THE LEVERS

No matter what the type or size of business you are in, there are really only a few levers when looking from fifty thousand feet. Looking at a high-level view of ANY income statement, you can see the same five major sections (indicated in the graphic below). Of those five major sections, three of those are your levers. No matter the income statement, it's always those three levers.

Income Statement Summary

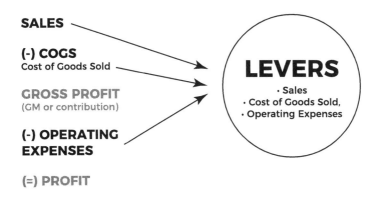

Said another way, looking at the simplified income statement above, in order to increase net profit, there are only three ways to do it:

1. Increase sales
2. Decrease COGS
3. Decrease operating expenses

Similarly, there are three levers on the balance sheet that can be pulled to help drive improved cash flow. Those levers are these:

1. Optimize accounts receivable
2. Turn inventory faster
3. Optimize accounts Payable

Notice that each of these levers are represented by a chart in the monthly reporting. Look back to exercise 1 in chapter 2 (charts review), and you'll see each chart is actually one of the levers (for those of you in manufacturing, you'll need your team to add a chart tracking inventory to your package). That's obviously by design so you can clearly understand what position each of the levers are in (i.e., good position or bad position). Looking back to chapter 2, exercise 2 (the Top 3 issues exercise) was designed to help you shine a light on which lever(s) needs to be pulled first (and the hardest).

1. HOW CAN WE INCREASE REVENUE?

There are two ways to increase revenue:

- **Increase prices.** Have you really maximized your pricing? Have you tested raising prices to see the result? Lots of entrepreneurs underprice their product or service. Don't be one of those leaving easy money on the table.
- **Increase throughput (a.k.a. volume).** There are a few ways to consider this.

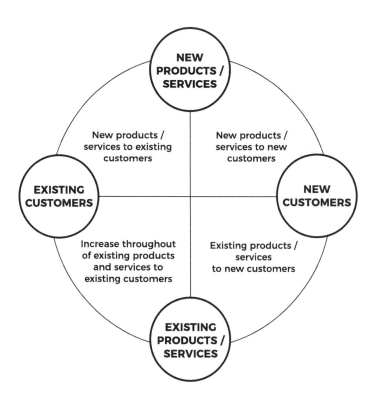

If sales is one of your Top 3 issues and you've already maximized price, have a look at the matrix above and figure out which has the best likelihood of increasing your throughput. By narrowing down a strategy, you can focus on key initiatives for that quadrant, increasing your likelihood of success.

2. HOW CAN WE INCREASE MARGIN?

The goal here is to reduce the cost of goods *or* hold it flat as sales increase (i.e., decreasing COGS as a percentage of sales as sales grow). For the vast majority of companies, COGS are almost entirely labor or materials, or a combination of both, with just a few percent in other stuff like supplies and freight. Given they are the majority of the COGS, labor and materials are the most obvious to tackle by asking the right questions, such as these:

- Our supplier just gave us a price increase. Can we do a competitive bid to reduce the cost of the key components in our product?
- Is there a process that is taking a long time that we could reengineer to reduce time and save labor and/or increase throughput with fewer labor hours?
- Which products/services/customers are making us the most money and which aren't? Can we adjust our sales mix to generate a better margin (i.e., reducing COGS)?

The other critical area to evaluate is rework. What mistakes are happening in the production/delivery/services in the business that are having to be redone, thereby wasting time and/or materials to keep the clients happy? This number can be surprisingly high to companies who aren't tracking it.

3. HOW CAN WE REDUCE OVERHEAD EXPENSES?

Again, this is either reduce expenses or hold steady with sales growth so they become less as a percentage of sales.

Two areas to focus on here:

1. **Costs under your control.** Some costs, like rent if you've signed a five-year lease with a personal guarantee, are really hard to impact. Focus on the ones that you directly control, like admin wages and travel (did someone say video conference?).
2. **Largest amounts first.** There is obviously more leverage in an area you're spending $87,673 a year on versus one that you're spending $3,283 on. There is more fat to be cut and more savings to be had in the big numbers.

With these levers, you have targeted all key levers on the income statement driving profitability. Again, a good reporting package (covered in part 3) will help shine a light on which lever you need to focus on.

The next levers are good for driving cash flow on the balance sheet. The nerdy way of saying this is "being more efficient with your working capital." The less nerdy way is as follows:

4. HOW CAN WE OPTIMIZE ACCOUNTS RECEIVABLE?

This is about getting the money in your bank account on time rather than having it sit in your customers' bank accounts.

How? Collect faster from your clients by following up with calls and emails. It's really effective to call them a week before the bill is due to remind them and confirm there is nothing in the way of them paying on time. Alternatively, can you start taking deposits? Changing your payment terms to shorten them from net thirty to net fifteen? Offering an early payment discount? It might be tough with existing clients, so how about setting better payment expectations with new clients?

5. HOW CAN WE IMPROVE INVENTORY TURNS?

Here is the silent killer of many a manufacturing and distribution business. The objective here is to consume your inventory as fast as possible. Every dollar of inventory sitting on the floor is a dollar out of your bank account, regardless of how profitable you are. There are lots of highly profitable manufacturing businesses that go under because their inventory is too high.

The lever comes down to this question: how can you "turn" or consume your inventory faster? Smaller purchases? Consignment inventory from suppliers? Implement lean manufacturing? Change your product mix? Eliminate items that generate low sales but require specialized components that sit a long time? Whatever the mechanism, pulling the inventory lever will free up cash for any manufacturing business. If you're in manufacturing, this one probably needs to be pulled the hardest.

6. HOW CAN WE OPTIMIZE ACCOUNTS PAYABLE?

Basically, you're trying to slow down payments to suppliers without upsetting them. One suggestion is to call your suppliers and ask for longer payment terms. If you are at net thirty, maybe ask for net sixty? You just might end up at net forty-five, giving yourself an extra fifteen days to pay. If you don't ask, you don't get.

Alternatively, set up a program with your payables clerk/bookkeeper to start paying ten days after the due date. Then twelve days, then fifteen days. Keep stretching until you start getting calls, then pull it back in a bit. The goal is to figure out the latest date you can pay without getting a phone call (even keep a schedule by supplier). It's money in the bank. Literally!

WHAT ABOUT THINGS LIKE EQUIPMENT AND DEBT?

Of course, there are other aspects of the balance sheet that you need to keep an eye on, such as capital spending, deposits, and debt levels. But the real drivers for most businesses are the levers identified in this chapter, and that's where you should be focusing most of your energy.

If you do have lots of capital equipment or debt, feel free to add it to your charts reporting package and keep an eye on those big numbers! More on that in the next section.

WHICH LEVER SHOULD YOU PULL?

Now that you've identified the potential levers, the question is, which one do you pull to get the most impact? Let your reporting package be your guide! In part 3, we will review in detail what a great monthly reporting package looks like and how it shines a light on the key levers and insights of the business.

PART 3

A COMPLETE REPORTING PACKAGE

This section of the book is your guide to what a great financial reporting package looks like and the necessary steps you (read: your accountant) can take to get it there.

Why does your reporting package matter so much? You need a package that addresses both the **Insights** (for you) and the **Hygiene** (not for you) in a single package. More specifically, you need a package that works for you (intuitive, quick, provides insights, and identifies the levers) *and* for the sophisticated users of your financial information (detailed financial statements in "accountant" or "banker" format) so you don't get in a bind when you really need it.

For your reporting packages, instruct your team to follow two very basic rules:

1. They are delivered at the same time.
2. They contain the same reports (unless updates or changes are being made).

Why? For both rules, the reason is the same: you don't want to have to remember to ask for it. It's too easy to get caught up in other things happening in the business and have the financials slip through the cracks. Don't accept your accountant waiting for you to ask for your package or specify which reports you want. The standing order is

"I want to see the monthly package by the tenth of every month."[14]

> **Note:** This section is only designed to give you a vision for the ideal monthly reporting package. The details and how are in part 4: The Hygiene Roadmap.

---

14 Or whatever day is practical in your business. The tenth is generally more than reasonable. Your accountants had better have a really, really good reason if they can't get it to you by the fifteenth.

CHAPTER 4

AN OVERVIEW OF YOUR MONTHLY FINANCIAL PACKAGE

Once you've reviewed this section, you will be able to give very specific directions to your team as to what you want included in your financial package (which, again, should be delivered to you by the tenth of each month). The following is a high-level overview of the package followed by more detailed instructions on the contents of each section. Head to Entrepreneumbers.com for a free download of a complete sample monthly reporting package to help put these instructions in better context.

The order of this package is laid out very intentionally. Looking at the reporting package summary, you can see the following sections:

1. **Charts.** This allows you to simply and intuitively under-

stand your current financial position and an overview of the levers.

2. **Top 3 Insights.** This allows you to simply and intuitively understand the key financial issues facing your business (and which issues you can set aside for now) and which levers you need to focus on pulling.

3. **Insights Analysis Backup.** This allows you (if you want) to dig a bit deeper into the Top 3 Insights to understand the lever and start to brainstorm how to course correct.

4. **Quarterly Review.** These are reports that are worth looking at once a quarter. Feel free to do it monthly, but only if you like diving into this stuff.

5. **Pure Hygiene reports.** This is here for the accountants and bankers. Again, feel free to dive in as much as you like. You may even want to (and dare I say, look forward to) as you get more and more comfortable with your numbers, but the whole point of this package is you don't *have* to. You'll get everything you need from the other sections, which are written for you in your language.

Monthly Reporting Package Summary

Charts - Understand Current Financial Position

Cashflow forecast	☐
Chart	☐
Detail	☐
Net income	☐
Month	☐
YTD	☐
Sales	☐
Month	☐
YTD	☐
Margin	☐
Month	☐
YTD	☐
Operation expense	☐
Month	☐
YTD	☐
AR days, pie, detail	☐
AP days, pie, detail	☐
Breakeven	☐
Custom charts for your business or industry	☐

Top 3 Insights / Key Observations

Write up	☐
Chart	☐

Insights Analysis Backup

Budget variance analysis ($ and %)	☐
Prior year variance analysis ($ and %)	☐
Profitability drivers analysis	☐
Segment	☐
80 / 20 rule	☐
Size	☐
Other	☐
Labor efficiency	☐
Dashboard	☐
Benchmark	☐
Ratio analysis	☐

Core Financials (Hygiene)

Income statement budget vs actuals - month	☐
Income statement budget vs actuals - year	☐
Income statement by month - YTD	☐
Balance sheet by month for fiscal year and last year	☐
Other industry report (i.e. inventory report, WIP report)	☐

Quarterly Review

Reoccurring charges (aka unused gym membership)	☐
General ledger by manager	☐

CHAPTER 5

———

MONTHLY CHARTS

At this point in the book, I've already told you ad nauseam how important your charts are. There's no sense beating a dead horse and telling you again, so let's get to it.

FIRST (AND ALWAYS FIRST): CASH FLOW FORECAST

The top half of the page is the chart or graphical representation of your future cash flow. In less than ten seconds, you'll obviously see if you are facing any cash shortfalls in the coming months, rather than finding out about it two days before payroll is due.

The second part is more for your bookkeeper, but it's also a tool for you. It's the backup calculation of the cash flow forecast. It's there for when you are seeing a crash in cash flow and you (and your accountant) can use the table to push and pull the numbers to manage your cash flow. Showing negative cash flow three months out? Can you push out a few payments? Can you get on the phone and call in a few receivables? What else can you do? That table is designed to help you manage through your short-term shortfalls. With this one report in place, you're well on your way to empowerment.

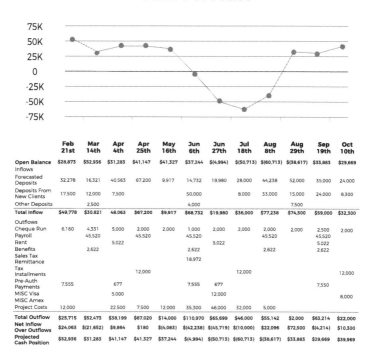

Cash Forecast

	Feb 21st	Mar 14th	Apr 4th	Apr 25th	May 16th	Jun 6th	Jun 27th	Jul 18th	Aug 8th	Aug 29th	Sep 19th	Oct 10th
Open Balance	$28,873	$52,936	$31,283	$41,147	$41,327	$37,244	$(4,994)	$(50,713)	$(60,713)	$(38,617)	$33,883	$29,669
Inflows												
Forecasted Deposits	32,278	16,321	40,563	67,200	9,917	14,732	19,980	28,000	44,238	52,000	35,000	24,000
Deposits From New Clients	17,500	12,000	7,500			50,000		8,000	33,000	15,000	24,000	8,300
Other Deposits		2,500				4,000				7,500		
Total Inflow	$49,778	$30,821	48,063	$67,200	$9,917	$68,732	$19,980	$36,000	$77,238	$74,500	$59,000	$32,300
Outflows												
Cheque Run	6,160	4,331	5,000	2,000	2,000	1,000	2,000	2,000	2,000	2,000	2,500	2,000
Payroll		45,520		45,520		45,520			45,520		45,520	
Rent			5,022				5,022				5,022	
Benefits		2,622				2,622			2,622		2,622	
Sales Tax Remittance						18,972						
Tax Installments				12,000				12,000				12,000
Pre-Auth Payments	7,555		677			7,555	677				7,550	
MISC Visa			5,000				12,000					
MISC Amex												8,000
Project Costs	12,000		22,500	7,500	12,000	35,300	46,000	32,000	5,000			
Total Outflow	$25,715	$52,473	$38,199	$67,020	$14,000	$110,970	$65,699	$46,000	$55,142	$2,000	$63,214	$22,000
Net Inflow Over Outflows	$24,063	$(21,652)	$9,864	$180	$(4,083)	$(42,238)	$(45,719)	$(10,000)	$22,096	$72,500	$(4,214)	$10,300
Projected Cash Position	$52,936	$31,283	$41,147	$41,327	$37,244	$(4,994)	$(50,713)	$(60,713)	$(38,617)	$33,883	$29,669	$39,969

NOTE: I get that the examples in this book are a bit small due to page size limitations. But I still wanted to include them so you can get a visual picture of what is described here. If you're looking to actually dig into the numbers, it's probably best you get the download. You can find a free download of both this chart and examples of the rest of the monthly reporting package at Entreprenumbers.com.

THE REST OF THE MONTHLY CHARTS

This visual representation of your financial results makes it so you don't have to grind through the detailed financial statements if you don't want to. I recommend the following charts (at a minimum) because these charts line up exactly with the levers identified in part 2:

- Net income (monthly result and year-to-date results in separate charts) comparing the following:
  - Current result
  - Last year result for the same period
  - Budget for the same period

Net Income - Month

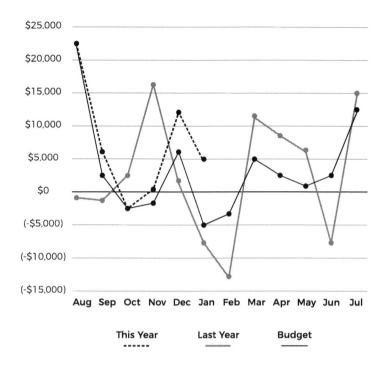

- Sales (same format as net income)[15] [16]
- Gross margin (same format as net income)
- Overhead expenses (same format as net income)
- Accounts receivable aging
  - Trend of days outstanding this year compared to last year

---

15   The order of what you are looking at is cash first (cash is king), net income (profit) second, and sales third. Don't get caught up on your top line sales. Your cash and profit might suck.

16   I could put in more charts here for sales, gross margin, overhead expenses, etc. But, seeing as they are already in part 1 and they're all showing you the same basic idea, I figured I wouldn't bore you here. If you're curious about what each individual chart looks like (and flipping back to part 1 is simply too much to bear), head over to Entreprenumbers.com for the full download.

- Pie chart showing the breakdown of overdue accounts[17]
- Detail of outstanding AR by customer (in case you need to dive into the details because of what you've seen in the charts)

Accounts Receivable Report

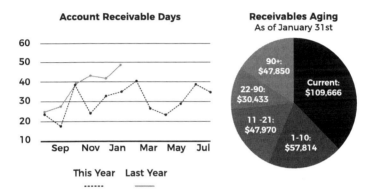

Account Receivable Days

Receivables Aging
As of January 31st

- 90+: $47,850
- Current: $109,666
- 22-90: $30,433
- 11-21: $47,970
- 1-10: $57,814

This Year   Last Year

Receivables	Current	1-10	11-21	22-90	90+	Total
Client 1	210					210
Client 2	467					467
Client 3	1,800	1,800				3,600
Client 4	3,675	2,800				6,475
...						
Client 20			18,432		26,142	44,574
Client 21				8,782		8,782
Client 22				279		279
Client 23					3,150	3,150
Client 24					12,338	12,338
Total	**$109,666**	**$57,814**	**$47,970**	**$30,433**	**$47,850**	**$293,732**

---

17 My preference for this chart is to run the number based on the date the report is run, *not* month end. If a bunch of collections are received after month end, no need getting worked up about an issue that is no longer relevant.

- Accounts payable aging
- Trend of days outstanding this year compared to last year
- Pie chart showing the breakdown of overdue accounts[18]
- Detail of outstanding AP by supplier/vendor (again, if you need to dig into the details based on what you see in the charts)

Accounts Payable Report

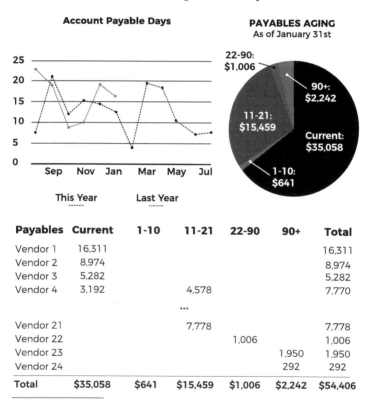

Account Payable Days

PAYABLES AGING
As of January 31st

This Year
Last Year

Payables	Current	1-10	11-21	22-90	90+	Total
Vendor 1	16,311					16,311
Vendor 2	8,974					8,974
Vendor 3	5,282					5,282
Vendor 4	3,192		4,578			7,770
			...			
Vendor 21			7,778			7,778
Vendor 22				1,006		1,006
Vendor 23					1,950	1,950
Vendor 24					292	292
Total	$35,058	$641	$15,459	$1,006	$2,242	$54,406

18 See previous note.

- Inventory turns
  - Average inventory turns for the month compared to prior year same period
  - Average inventory turns for the quarter compared to prior year same period
- Breakeven analysis[19]
  - Breakeven by month compared to prior year same period
  - Breakeven by quarter (or year) compared to prior year same period to smooth out the bumps in the road.
- Other custom charts that are relevant for your business or industry. Focus on the largest line item, areas you want to focus on, or line items specific to your business such as these:
  - Work in progress
  - Gross margin of your largest segment
  - Debt load (if you are focused on reducing debt)
  - Total labor

After reviewing these charts (which should only take a few minutes), you should have a clear picture of your current

---

19   Virtually every entrepreneur I know asks the same question: "How much do I have to sell in order to cover my monthly nut?" Every quarter, ask your accountant for a quick and dirty breakeven analysis. You'll know when you need to hit in sales to break even as you make changes to your business. Hired a new salesperson? That changes your breakeven. Found ways to improve your gross margin? That changes your breakeven. Moved to a new office? That likely changes your breakeven. Tracking your breakeven though charts is one of the most clarifying things you can do for your business (and mental health).

financial position and the state of your key levers, at least at a high level.

CHAPTER 6

TOP 3 INSIGHTS

This is the fun part—the moment where you start to get clarity on the most pressing issues in your business. Now that it's time to review your Top 3 issues, here's what to expect.

KEY OBSERVATIONS FOR THE MONTH

The key observations is a quick narrative of the most important items of note from this month's results, **rank ordered by impact on cash and/or impact on profit.** This narrative is derived from the Top 3 chart described in the next section. Think bullet points, not some long narrative that no one wants to read—and no spewing numbers that can be easily be seen in the charts. This is giving you the *context* around the key issues facing the business.

TOP 3 ISSUES CHART RANK ORDERED BY IMPACT ON CASH AND/OR IMPACT ON PROFIT

This might become one of your favorite things to look at: the key issues of your business in a simple, easy-to-understand chart with a short narrative on each of the top 3 items. While this chart looks simple and easy, it's not that simple for your team to pull together.

Key Observations for the Month

#1 Job Size. Of the ninety-seven jobs we completed this year, fifty-seven were "small" jobs. Because of the cost of running and managing these jobs, on average they cost the company around $1,500 per job. The total impact of these jobs is over $90,000 annualized.

#2 Labor Creep. Labor as a percentage of sales has increased by almost 4 percent over the past couple of years. If we were able to hold labor to the same rate we were at a couple of years ago, we would be spending $80,000 annualized less than we are right now.

#3 Accounts Receivable. Our AR collections are slow with over half of our receivables being overdue. If we collected at even a reasonable pace (not perfect), we would have about $40,000 more cash in the bank right now.

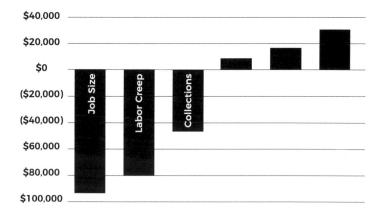

Top 3 Insights

There are several different analyses that need to get done for this chart to be of value, and each one has to be rank ordered by impact on cash or impact on profit. For that, you'll need the...

CHAPTER 7

———

INSIGHTS ANALYSIS BACKUP

The Insights Analyses are all of the different calculations and analyses your team will have to do in order to come up with the Top 3. There is no quick-and-easy way to do this (until AI analysis gets a little better). To get this right, it's a combination of knowing what types of analysis to do for the industry, what types of analysis to do for the business, how to calculate them, and how to integrate them.

Again, this book is not an accounting lesson. The expectation is that you have the resources in place to handle this type of work and you will hold your team accountable for getting it done. If your team isn't up for it, there are some suggestions for you near the end of part 4.

ANALYSES EVERY COMPANY SHOULD BE DOING

Like the title says, these are analyses that every company should be doing. This means regardless of industry or sector.

BUDGET VARIANCE ANALYSIS

Comparing the actual performance against your budget (both monthly and year to date).

This report is simple to complete. For instance, if you budgeted your labor at $50,000 but your actual labor is $120,000, then you know you've got a $70,000 problem there. If that $70,000 represents the largest gap between budget and actuals, then that's the problem you'll want to focus on first.

Have your bookkeeper review each line of the income statement and rank order the Top 5 line item offenders that are worse than budget and chart them in a simple bar chart.[20] You can also rank order to Top 5 success against budget so you know what is also going well.[21]

Top 5 Budget Variance

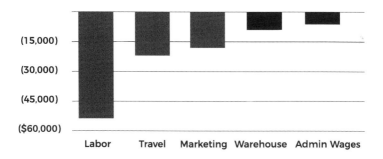

Labor	Travel	Marketing	Warehouse	Admin Wages

---

20   While the goal is to identify the Top 3 overall financial issues for the company, your team can cast the net a bit wider to rank ordering the Top 5 issues from each analysis. Chapter 9 will explain how to narrow down all these Top 5 issues into the overall Top 3.

21   For more on setting up budget, see chapter 13.

Top 5 with Positive

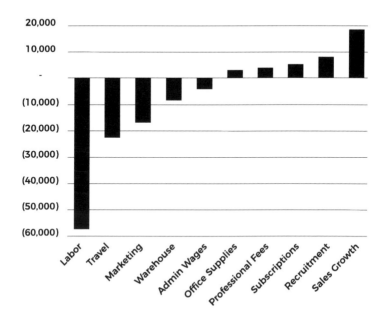

PRIOR YEAR VARIANCE ANALYSIS

What are the worst trends you've seen over the past few years? Personally, I think the conversation begins and ends with Segways, man-buns, and Kardashians. They serve no purpose, nobody likes them, and you look silly if you're seen with one.

This analysis will help root out the Segways, man-buns, and Kardashians in your business by comparing the actual performance against your prior year (both monthly and year to date).

This is simple to complete and is the exact same process as the budget variance analysis above, rank ordering the Top 5 offenders that are tracking worse than last year (and potentially the five tracking better than last year) and putting them on a simple, intuitive chart for you.

Top 5 Prior Year Variances

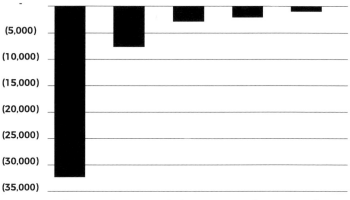

	Labor	Meals & Ent.	Admin Wages	Warehouse	Recruitment

(5,000)
(10,000)
(15,000)
(20,000)
(25,000)
(30,000)
(35,000)

TO ACCOUNTANTS

One important note here. Similar to the budget variance analysis, this needs to be done both in gross dollars and also indexed to sales in order to get the whole story.

You may have already noticed that the recruitment bar is showing positive in the "budget" variance chart and negative in the "prior year" variance chart. Great job! Yes, in this case, recruitment is over budget, but less than last year. So what? The whole point of doing multiple Insights Analyses is bringing certainty to your overall Top 3 by not being misled by one single analysis. See chapter 9 for pulling all the analyses together.

When these first two simple analyses are complete, you'll have a clear picture of where you might be going off track. Simple to put together and powerful data. But don't stop there.

ANALYSES THAT WILL VARY BY COMPANY AND INDUSTRY

There are a number of other analyses that need to be done in order to get really clear on the Top 5. These will vary company by company, and lots of thought needs to be put in to figuring out which ones are relevant for you. Some conversations with gray-haired advisors would be a good idea here.

PROFITABILITY ANALYSIS BY SEGMENT/CUSTOMER TYPE/SIZE/ETC.

While the exact analysis depends on your business, the crux is having your team slice and dice the data and rank order which parts are making the most money (and which are losing the most). Some options for analysis include these:

1. **Profitability by segment.** Looking at your business, consider what parts of the business operate differently and rank order the segments by margin percent as well as total contribution dollars earned. You may discover that your best margin segment is also your smallest by sales and is begging to be scaled.

2. **Profitability by customer.** Again, rank order your customers by contribution dollars and margin percent. Then have your team look for an 80/20(ish) rule. Are your top 20 percent of customers earning 80 percent of your revenue? Are you spending a bunch of time and resources on a bunch of clients who aren't really making you much money?

3. **Profitability by location.** If you have more than one location, compare locations and see which ones are the most profitable.

As usual, each of these analyses need to be converted to the impact on cash or profit. If you find location one and two are way more profitable than location three, how much is it costing in profit to have an underperforming location?

Once your team has applied their super-secret accounting magic to your different profitability analyses, you will end up with a clear picture of which parts of your business are the most profitable and which of your products or services are actually costing you money rather than making you money. Once they are rank ordered and put on a simple intuitive chart, you'll know exactly how to drive increased profitability into the business.

Profitability Analysis

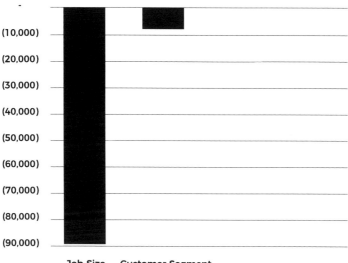

	Job Size	Customer Segment
(10,000)		
(20,000)		
(30,000)		
(40,000)		
(50,000)		
(60,000)		
(70,000)		
(80,000)		
(90,000)		

TO ENTREPRENEURS AND ACCOUNTANTS

You'll notice that there isn't actually a Top 5 here. That's OK. Some of these analyses may only result in one or two numbers. Don't get hung up on making each analysis have five results. Sometimes you may only need to examine profitability a couple of ways to really drive out the issues. For example, if you only have one type of product that you're selling out of one location, you might look at profitability by customer type or average sale size, but there is no segmenting to be done by location or product type. The key here is to get clear on the profitability drivers and rank order those by impact on profit or impact on cash.

LABOR EFFICIENCY

Almost every single business should be analyzing labor. Unless you're in manufacturing or retail, labor is almost certainly your number-one expense. For a somewhat exaggerated example, just look at any professional sports team. Most of their money is tied up in those multimillion-dollar contracts they hand out to their players. Sure, they have other expenses (those lush green lawns don't fertilize, seed, and water themselves, you know), but none are so great as what they're spending on their star employees.

There are a few different ways to look at and analyze your labor depending on your type of business, and the specific analysis depends on your business. Some options for analysis include these:

- Labor utilization (What percent of the time is your labor working on "productive" activities?)
- Labor utilization by individual
- Labor efficiency ratio (your revenue/total labor) to see how much your labor is contributing to the business
- Revenue (or contribution dollar) by count of full-time equivalent

There are lots of ways to measure labor efficiency. Whatever the method of measuring, again, have your team convert the impact to cash or profit. You might have a 73 percent labor utilization compared to last year of 76 percent and a budget of 75 percent. What is that 2 percent shortfall really costing you? If it turns out to be one of your Top 3, then you know what to focus on. If it turns out that 2 percent is a relatively small problem compared to your other issues, shelve it for now and come back to it when you've gotten the big problems sorted.

DASHBOARD ANALYSIS

You have a dashboard, right? If not, see the appendix for a brief overview on setting one up.

When you do have it set up, like the rest of the Insights Analysis, it's critical to convert the dashboard into impact on cash or impact on profit. Here's why: Imagine one of your metrics is sales growth. You have a target of 20 percent growth, but you actually only hit 18 percent, missing by 2 percent. Imagine you also have a metric of labor utilization with a target of 75 percent, but you actually hit only 73 percent, again missing by 2 percent. Which is the bigger issue—sales or labor?

The answer? It depends.

Specifically, it depends on which problem has a bigger impact on cash or profit. Running the math, your accountant *needs* to deliver your dashboard analysis (and all the other analyses) rank-ordered by *impact on cash* or *impact on profit*. In this example, if your sales metric (that you missed by 2 percent) is costing you $18,000 of profit, while your labor metric (that you also missed by 2 percent) is costing you $87,000, then it's painfully obvious which is the bigger issue and which issue you should be focused on. The same goes for *all* of the analyses noted earlier.

So, have your team rank order your dashboard based on impact on cash or impact on profit and put it in a simple, intuitive chart. You can see you are building a collection of these top impact charts. Don't worry, at the end of part 3, we'll distill it down into one intuitive and simple Top 3 Insights chart.

TO ACCOUNTANTS

Because of the nature of certain metrics, you may not be able to convert all of them back to cash or profit for the Top 3 analysis. Don't panic. Rank the metrics that *can* be converted while being aware of those that can't.

For instance, in a call center, you could convert the number of calls to the impact on cash, especially if you knew the conversion ratio for your average client. Say a call center is ten calls short of their target. Because they close two of every ten calls, they miss out on two sales. If each sale is worth $500, the company would miss out on $1,000 worth of revenue at a 20 percent profit margin. That day, in other words, $200 was left on the table.

CHAPTER 8

_____

MORE SOPHISTICATED ANALYSES (WHEN YOU'RE READY FOR THEM)

I'm an ultra-distance athlete. Over the years, I've built up a list of accomplishments that look pretty good on paper:

- I won the first triathlon I was ever in.
- I came in second in the Vancouver 100K trail run.
- I'm tied for the all-time record in the 22K Squamish Scrambler trail run.
- I came tenth in the "All Hallows Eve" trail marathon.

Sounds pretty great, doesn't it? Out of context, they certainly are. However, the real story behind each is much more humbling. For instance:

- The first triathlon I did was called "My First Triathlon" and was exclusively designed for first-time triathletes.

As a seasoned marathoner, I was also training for Iron-man that year and, while legitimately never having done a triathlon, was riding a fully kitted-out triathlon bike I bought for Ironman and was competing against people mostly riding mountain bikes—some with knobby tires, and some with baskets on the front (insert slap on the forehead emoji).

· The Vancouver 100K is a club run, not a race. Only about a dozen people participated, and most of us were all running all together for virtually the entire run. With about thirty minutes left to go, a few people stopped to grab a snack. I would have stopped too, but I felt like crap and wanted to be done with it, so I kept going. The people who stopped for a snack whom I "beat" typically finish hours ahead of me in ultra-marathons. The guy who "won" finished a full seven hours ahead of me (yes, seven hours!).

· The year I set the Squamish Scrambler record (also a club run, not a true "race"), there were phenomenally low levels of snow. It was the first time in the history of the event that we could run the entire 22K without using snowshoes—which, in case you didn't know, slow you down quite a bit. In an actual snowshoe run, I wouldn't have come close to setting the record.

· The All Hallows Eve Marathon had thirty-six total entrants. I came tenth, a typical top-third(ish) finish, but by no means an elite performance. If three hundred people had raced, I would have placed right around eightieth, which doesn't sound nearly as exciting.

The lesson here is that context matters. Sure, I can use numbers to paint a pretty picture of my accomplishments (and you can likely do that with your business too), but that pretty picture isn't grounded in any reality. I'd be fooling myself if I identified as an elite athlete. I'm usually just a few steps ahead of average. An "elite mid-packer," if you will.

Entrepreneurs are optimistic by nature. We have to be, given the uncertainty of our work. But optimism is no excuse for wearing rose-colored glasses. We need to know where we *really* stand in relation to other businesses in our industry. The more analysis you have done on your business, the more confident you can be that you're heading in the right direction. The following are some additional analyses for you to get your team to add once you've mastered the ones above.

BENCHMARK ANALYSIS

By comparing yourself to similar businesses—just like we compared my accomplishments to those of other runners to begin this chapter—you develop a better understanding of your own performance relative to others. Benchmark data can be accessed from a few different sources, the most common of which are your banker (who has access to various sources of benchmark data) and other commercial data aggregators. You can look online to see who has data in your industry and region. Your banker will likely share industry-specific data if you ask for it. What's good for you is usually good for them. The commercial options, will, for a fee, give you access to benchmark data specific to your industry code. The data are organized by company size and sales, and then broken down further into quarters based on performance—top, top-middle, bottom-middle, and bottom.

Most benchmark data are broken down into income statement, balance sheet, and ratio data (see next section for more on ratios). Again, this gets much more complicated, so you'll need a more sophisticated team to pull it together for you.

As always, after they grind out the numbers, have them (say it with me) put together a simple, intuitive chart rank ordering the Top 5 issues by impact on cash or impact on profit.

Benchmark

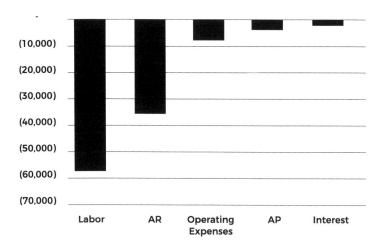

	Labor	AR	Operating Expenses	AP	Interest

(10,000)
(20,000)
(30,000)
(40,000)
(50,000)
(60,000)
(70,000)

YOUR BUSINESS CATEGORY MIGHT NOT BE A PERFECT FIT

When looking at the data for other businesses in your category, take the information with a grain of salt. Your company might not fall perfectly into any one of the comparative categories. For example, you might get a category for custom home builders, but it may be that your company is more of a hybrid. You build some custom homes, spec some homes, some commercial units, and tenant improvements. In such a case, your company will touch on several categories, but not be a perfect fit for any single one, making it even more difficult to collect and analyze data. The result is still worth reviewing for any major insights as long as you don't get too hung up on the more generalized data.

RATIO ANALYSIS

As an entrepreneur, you've probably applied for some form of financing during the life of your business. No matter where you go for a loan, the process is basically the same: you head to the bank, meet with an account or relationship manager, and present them with the necessary information. Your account manager then puts a proposal together and hands it off to the bank's internal risk assessment group, who gives the application a thumbs-up or a thumbs-down. There are all kinds of different names for these groups depending on the bank. But you'll never actually get to talk to them. Ever. I'm not sure they are actually human.

When applying for a loan, in other words, the person you spend all your time talking to has no decision-making power. You can charm your account manager all you want, which may help *a little*, but your fate lies squarely with a group of people you'll never speak to directly.

You may never meet your risk assessment group, but that doesn't mean you can't learn how to play their game. The trick is knowing what kind of information that group pays the most attention to. By knowing that, you can learn to paint your business in the best possible light.

So what *are* your lenders looking at? In a word, ratios. Sure, your story and your industry play a role, but the vast majority of the decision is based on your ratios. Your ratios show the health of your business. While certain ratios can paint a rosy picture of your financial standing, other ratios expose the problems lying underneath.

Ratios are just a different way to look at your financial statements by adding, subtracting, dividing, and multiplying certain line items on your financial statement together. For example:

"Current Ratio" = Current Assets / Current Liabilities

Or:

"Quick Ratio" = [Current Assets – Inventory] / Current Liabilities

The idea of this particular ratio is an indication of your ability to pay your upcoming bills in the relative short term. If your current assets are more than your current liabilities, it shows you are unlikely to have a major cash issue in the immediate future. If your current liabilities are more (or, way more) than your current assets, there is an increased risk that you will not be able to pay your bills on time, which means, no matter how charming you are, the risk assessment officer reviewing your file has already started reaching for their reject stamp. I always picture those people smiling when they reject a financing proposal. Those inhuman monsters!

If you aren't sure which ratios to pick, ask your banker for a list of ones they use (they should be happy to share), and/or look at the benchmark data you collected. Either is a great place to start.

Like benchmark analysis, ratio analysis is technically complex and beyond the scope of this book. But by now you get the deal. With the right team, you can also request your financial ratios rank ordered by impact on cash or impact on profit in a simple, intuitive chart.

TO ACCOUNTANTS

This is a complicated one. Aside from the complexity of just calculating your ratios, figuring out the impact on cash or profit is even more complicated. For this you'll need to set targets for the business based on either your budgets or industry benchmarks. Then, compare the company performance to those targets and calculate the impact on cash or profit. This is going to be the most technically challenging report to complete, so get everything else in place and come back to it at the end to really create a masterpiece!

IT DOESN'T STOP THERE

This is *not* a complete list. There are an unlimited number of analyses that can be done on a set of financials. If there are analyses you've learned from another source, by all means get your team to add them to the list. Of course, beware of analysis paralysis. The analysis suggested in this book will allow you to confidently uncover the stories buried in your financial statements so you don't get blindsided or get completely locked down in analysis paralysis.

BROKEN RECORD WARNING–MOST IMPORTANT PART

Every one of these analyses *must* be converted to *impact on cash* or *impact on profit*. Without this critical step, you'll just have a bunch of analyses that likely won't help you make a decision. Next is the last step of your Top 3 report.

CHAPTER 9

DECIDING ON YOUR OVERALL TOP 3

Now that you've completed the various Insights Analyses that are most relevant for your operation, you should have a bunch of Top 5 issues charts facing your business.[22] Now it's time for your accounting team to pull those issues together and determine the Top 3 *overall* issues facing your business.

To begin, your accountants will hand you a bunch of charts that look something like this:

----

22 Remember, some of these analyses will have five issues identified and some may have only one or two.

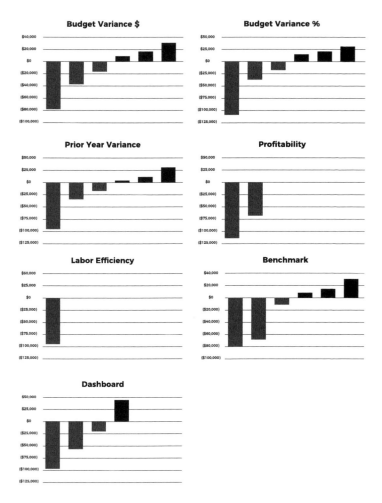

The next step is to consolidate your charts by combining, ranking, and debating the issues that have surfaced in the various analyses. It's up to you whether you want to be part of the consolidation process or want to sit this one out and just get the final Top 3 chart. Personally, I enjoy sitting in on the consolidation phase because it gives me a nice, broad picture of my business. And really, there's not much to it.

Consolidation goes something like this: Once you have your various analyses in front of you, you might notice that some issues repeat from analysis to analysis. For instance, multiple analyses might identify labor as an issue, albeit with slightly different values. Your dashboard analysis might put the issue at $60,000, the trends analysis might put it at $70,000, and your ratios analysis might put it at $80,000. It's OK if the numbers disagree—they were produced using different methodologies—but the takeaway here is that labor is clearly an issue. To create a set number value, just take the average of the three numbers and say labor is a $70,000 issue. If you have one outlier showing the labor issue at only $12,000, you and your team can use judgment either to average all of the numbers or to exclude the outlier.

Once everything is consolidated, your list of issues has been consolidated down, but it may still include as many as six to ten different issues. Now all you have to do is identify the three issues with the highest dollar values and circle them.

Just like that, you've identified the Top 3 issues facing your business and your accountant can provide your Top 3 Insights chart for the month.

Now comes the fun part: solving them.

Take a moment to review the overall list. Make sure the Top 3 issues intuitively make sense to you and are aligned with your gut. Your gut is probably pretty good. If the data is telling you something completely different than your gut, talk to your team about it. Share what your gut is telling you is the biggest issue and have your team dive back in and relook at the numbers. Just be open to the fact that there might actually be bigger issues than what your gut is telling you.

As stated in chapter 1, your books are dying to tell you a story. The Insights Analysis will reveal that story and empower you to make better decisions for your business without wading through pages and pages of accounting doublespeak. Once you've directed your accounting team to deliver you a monthly Insights report—and in a format that makes sense—you will have the advantage that so many other entrepreneurs crave: financial clarity.

TO ENTREPRENEURS AND BOOKKEEPERS

By now you should know the absolute crux of this exercise. Each of these analyses *must* be converted to *impact on cash* or *impact on profit*. Without this critical step, you'll just have a bunch of analyses that likely won't help you make a decision.

CHAPTER 10

CORE FINANCIAL (HYGIENE) REPORTS

This list will satisfy all sophisticated users of your financial statement (i.e., bankers, buyers, and other accountants):

1. Income statement actual vs. budget vs. prior year for:
   A. Current month
   B. Year to date
2. Income statement by month for the fiscal year
3. Balance sheet by month for the fiscal year and compared to last year same month
4. Other industry reports (i.e., inventory reports, WIP, etc.)

Since these reports fall into the Hygiene (not for you) category, you can find more details and examples about setting up these reports properly in part 4, The Hygiene Roadmap.

CHAPTER 11

QUARTERLY REPORTS

The quarterly reports fall into the "gross things I don't really want to do" pile. Admittedly, they are a bit more of a grind, which is why you only have to do them four times a year. If you hate it so much, feel free to make it twice a year and schedule it right after you go to the dentist. Then it won't feel so bad.

RECURRING CHARGES REPORT (A.K.A. THE UNUSED GYM MEMBERSHIP REPORT)

This one actually isn't so bad. Ask your accountant to put together a list of recurring charges, often paid by credit card. Think of all the subscription services you have signed up for. Are you still using all of them? Or have some slipped through the cracks and you've been paying $32.95 per month for a service you haven't used over the past year and a half (and haven't even logged into). While this book is generally focused on identifying and attacking the biggest financial issues facing the business, this is a five-minute exercise that often results in a few, small, easy wins.

	OCT	NOV	DEC	JAN
ADOBE CREATIVE CLOUD	904	850	935	765
ASANA	190	190	190	190
DROPBOX	32	32	32	32
GODADDY	87	65	23	62
RECEIPT BANK	40	40	40	40
ETC.				

GENERAL LEDGER REVIEW

Once a quarter, have your bookkeeper print out the general ledger detail for all expense items and hand them out (with a big smile) to whoever is responsible for those line items. If you have an ops manager, they should review all expense accounts falling under the operations department. Similarly, your sales manager should review the sales expenses, and so on. They need to do a quick review to make sure nothing got miscoded. Yes, a good accounting policy (which we'll talk about in part 4—The Hygiene Roadmap) should ensure that things are coded to the right spot. This is not only a double check, but it also holds your managers accountable for knowing what's *exactly* going into their budget lines (more on budgets in the Hygiene Roadmap section, as well). In fact, good managers should be *asking* for this detail, not fighting against doing this exercise.

5051 SUBSCRIPTIONS

11/1/2018	EXPENSE	AMAZON	19.11
11/1/2018	Bill	GoDaddy.com	11.99
11/3/2018	Bill	GoDaddy.com	46.10
11/5/2018	Expense	Everhour	9.00
11/6/2018	Expense	QuickBooks Online	30.93
11/8/2018	Expense	Amazon	207.89
11/8/2018	Expense	Amazon	33.78
11/8/2018	Expense	Amazon	18.89
11/9/2018	Expense	Google.com	2.79
11/10/2018	Expense	GoDaddy.com	36.07
11/14/2018	Expense	Microsoft	12.32
11/15/2018	Expense	Asana	407.62
1/14/2019	Expense	Dropbox	429.00
1/15/2019	Expense	Asana	489.96
1/16/2019	Expense	NationBuilder	39.48
1/20/2019	Expense	Everhour	238.28
1/22/2019	Expense	FormSite.com	34.20
1/25/2019	Expense	Zoom	211.83
TOTAL FOR SUBSCRIPTIONS			8,115.28

5111 OFFICE SUPPLIES

11/01/2018	Expense	Google.com	162.63
11/05/2018	Expense	iTunes	1.29
11/08/2018	Bill	VOIP	33.60
11/08/2018	Bill	Amazon	232.58
11/08/2018	Bill	Apple Store	84.00
1/16/2019	Bill	IKEA	79.00
1/24/2019	Expense	Apple Store	37.33
1/27/2019	Bill	Amazon	49.95
1/28/2019	Bill	Easykeyscom	36.74
1/31/2019	Expense	iTunes	13.43
TOTAL FOR 5111 OFFICE SUPPLIES			**3,665.93**

THE COMPLETE PACKAGE

That's your entire monthly reporting package. Wherever you sit on the empowerment curve today, you now have a clear vision of what an empowered reporting package looks like and feels like:

1. Clearly understand your current financial position.
2. Understand the Top 3 financial issues facing your business.
3. Clear your mind of the smaller issues that can wait until the large ones have been solved.
4. Brainstorm solutions to your big issues.

5. Complete within 15 minutes per month (unless you choose to dig deeper).

6. Do this all without ever having to look at an actual set of financial statements (and they are there if you want to dig in).

In part 4, The Hygiene Roadmap, we'll go over the details of how to take your reporting package from wherever it is now to where it needs to be.

TO ACCOUNTANTS

The owner of your business now has a clear vision of what to expect from you. If you're not delivering that now, or you don't know how to deliver it, read on to part 4, The Hygiene Roadmap, for details on getting the basics in place so you can deliver an awesome package each month. This is where the hard work really starts.

TO ENTREPRENEURS

You've got the full picture and a vision of empowerment. Now the hard work begins, getting solid accounting Hygiene in place. We shoved this section in the back of the book because I know you're never going to read it or do it yourself. That's OK. It's worth skimming over so you know how to hold your team accountable for getting it done and to know what good Hygiene actually looks like. Remember, you don't have to do any of this, but just make sure it gets done when you hand part 4 to your bookkeeper and say, "Go."

PART 4

THE HYGIENE
ROADMAP

Imagine you own a restaurant. Who uses your restroom most? It's not you—it's your customers and employees. Sure, you use the restroom from time to time too, but as far as appearances are concerned, it's there for *them*, not you.

Now, pretend you're one of those customers. You've just ordered dinner and excused yourself to use the restroom—only to be greeted by a disgusting, ill-maintained facility. *If this is what the restroom looks like*, you think to yourself, *then what about the kitchen?* Suddenly those shrimp kebabs and steamed mussels you ordered don't seem nearly so appetizing. By all appearances, this restaurant practices terrible hygiene.

Just as a quality restaurant *needs* to practice good hygiene with its bathrooms, a business *needs* to practice good Hygiene with its books. Like the restaurant, good Hygiene isn't for you. It's for the other users of your books:

1. **Bankers:** If you ever want to borrow or continue borrowing money, your bank will look at your accounting Hygiene.
2. **Buyer's advisors:** If you ever want to sell your business, your buyer's bankers and lawyers will look at your accounting Hygiene.
3. **Government bodies:** If you ever get audited by a tax authority like the IRS or Revenue Canada, those auditors will take an extra-long, uncomfortably close look

at your accounting Hygiene (think rubber-glove treatment).

With good Hygiene, whenever one of these sophisticated users looks at your books, you'll be ready to impress. After all, first impressions are everything. As soon as they see that your Hygiene is great, it's a signal to them that your "kitchen" is in great shape too. Never underestimate the power of showing great financial Hygiene to one of those groups. For instance, even if your numbers aren't anything to write home about when applying for a loan, the bankers will see that you have your shit together and will be more likely to go to bat for you and encourage the risk assessment group to support your application (within reasonable limits, of course).

Don't forget that like the owner of a restaurant using the restroom, you are *also* a consumer of your accounting Hygiene. The difference is you won't use it the same way as the other users. For you, good accounting Hygiene informs the Insights and Insights Analysis we looked at in the last section of the book.

The following graphic shows the key elements of the Hygiene Roadmap, which we'll cover one by one in the following chapters. Use this image as a checklist to see what parts of the roadmap you are on top of and what parts need work. The closer you get to ticking all the boxes, the closer you'll be to being on top of your Hygiene.

Hygiene Road Map

Financial Reporting

Financial statement presentation ☐
- o Income statement by accountability areas ☐
- o Descending by account size ☐
- o Account groupings and size ☐
- o Chart of accounts reviewed by CPA in the last two years ☐

Annual budget in place ☐

Hygiene reporting documents
Monthly reports
- o Cash flow projections (weekly if cash flow is an issue) ☐
- o Income statement by month ☐
- o Income statement budget vs. actual - month ☐
- o Income statement budget vs. actual - YTD ☐
- o Balance sheet by month ☐
- o AR aging report ☐
- o AP aging report ☐
- o Industry specific report (i.e. summary of job profitability) ☐

Quarterly reports
- o Recurring charges ☐
- o General ledger by management area ☐
☐

Process & Procedures

Primary work flow
- o Prospecting ☐
- o Closing ☐
- o Onboarding ☐
- o Execution ☐
- o Exit ☐

Accounting ☐
- o Revenue and collections ☐
  - · Invoicing ☐
  - · AR collections ☐
- o Expenses and payments ☐
  - · PO approval ☐
  - · Invoice approval ☐
  - · Account coding and allocation ☐

HR
- o Employee expense submission and approval ☐
- o Employee onboarding ☐
- o Employee Status change and offboarding ☐
- o Vacation policy and tracking ☐

Annual Close
- o Year end ☐
- o Taxes ☐

Software

Cloud based, automated system implemented & functional for:
- o Accounting software ☐
- o Expense tracking/management ☐
- o Payroll processing ☐
- o Invoicing ☐
- o Task/Project Management ☐
- o EFT - Payment and collections processing ☐
- o Time Tracking ☐
- o Industry Specific (i.e. Quoting, POS, etc) ☐

Task Management

Related task list for accountant
- o Daily ☐
- o Weekly ☐
- o Monthly ☐
- o Quarterly ☐
- o Annually ☐

CHAPTER 12

———

FINANCIAL REPORTING

Since we already covered the overview of the entire reporting package, this chapter is about the details needed to get it right. This includes how it's set up and some of the other subtleties that the sophisticated users will really appreciate.

GETTING IT RIGHT

GROUP YOUR INCOME STATEMENT BY ACCOUNTABILITY AREA

Setting up your income statement by accountability area is a game changer as you grow and build your management team. Looking at your current income statement, are all the expenses in one big long list? Are they grouped together in ways that don't make sense?

If you answered yes to either of those, it's time to ask your accountant to reformat your income statement along the lines of accountability. Have an R&D department with an

R&D manager? Group all costs associated with R&D under a subheading of R&D. Have an admin or office manager? Group all admin or office-related costs under an admin subheading. Same with sales and any other main departments you have.

Operating Expenses

G&A EXPENSES	JANUARY	DECEMBER	YTD
Payroll salaries general	18,782	19,188	37,971
Accounting and legal	1,946	2,029	6,419
Other expense	4,770	0	4,770
Computer and internet	984	1,380	4,019
Telephone	465	380	2,134
Training	53	102	156
Payroll expense	18	19	38
TOTAL G&A EXPENSES	**$29,539**	**$25,509**	**$63,676**
Ops expenses			
Consulting	5,323	5,784	19,759
Tooling, setup, and other	3,264	0	4,909
Freight, duty, and brokerage	41	0	66
TOTAL OPS EXPENSES	**$8,629**	**$5,784**	**$24,735**
R&D expenses			
Consulting	5,958	6,089	17,748
Tooling, setup, and other	46	277	1,798
Freight, duty, and brokerage	21	39	414
Software	25	25	75
TOTAL R&D EXPENSES	**$6,051**	**$6,432**	**$20,036**

Why? Because when you set a budget (more on this later), you can now hold your managers accountable for staying within budget. Push down the financial responsibility of the area onto them! You'll still get high-level overview of the financials, but your team will now be responsible for getting into the detailed accounts. Look back at the reporting package summary and the quarterly task G/L review task. This is exactly what that report is for. You'll be able to easily see which one of your managers is running a tight department and who has costs going out of control.

☐ **Tick the Box:** You get to tick this box as complete when you look at your income statement and the expense accounts are grouped into your main departments and those groups make intuitive sense based on your business.

Note: The examples shown in this section (and those that follow) are short-form excerpts from a complete package. You can download an example of an entire report from Entreprenumbers.com.

ORDER YOUR INCOME STATEMENT–FROM LARGEST TO SMALLEST

You've probably run out of memory on your smartphone at least once. When this happens, most operating systems make fixing the problem simple by showing us exactly which apps are using the most memory, starting with the worst offenders. At the top of the list might be your photos app (60 percent of memory), followed by video downloads (30 percent), e-books (4 percent), and so on, until you're down to the minor offenders—smaller apps that take up a tiny fraction of 1 percent of memory.

Now ask yourself, if you're trying to free up memory, which apps do you tackle first? Obviously look at the photos and the video downloads, which are clearly creating the biggest burden on your total available memory.

Your financial statements should be organized in the same way. Direct your accounting team to sort your expenses within each subheader from largest to smallest. It's likely the 80/20 rule applies here: the first few lines of your statement will likely cover 80 percent of your expenses.

Look at the table in the previous section and note how each line item is sorted from largest line item to smallest within each section.

Two good reasons for doing this:

First, as you get more comfortable with your financial package and when (or if) you choose to start spending more time on your financials, you'll start by looking at the biggest line items rather than working through all the noise.

Second, if you're feeling tired or lazy during your review, you'll still see all the most important stuff before your attention drifts off (squirrel!).

It's very similar to rank ordering the Top 3 Insights. Focus on the biggest stuff first and get rid of the rest of the noise.

- ☐ **Tick the Box:** You get to tick this box as complete when you see that your biggest expenses show up at the top of each section of the income statement.

MAKE THE STATEMENT AS SHORT AS POSSIBLE

If you're running a massive multinational corporation like General Electric, then your financial statements are necessarily long and complex, dragging on with lots of schedules and subschedules. But you're not running a corporation like General Electric. Your company is relatively straightforward by comparison. Since you're only doing a fraction of the business GE is, it stands to reason that your financial statement should only be a fraction as long.

Direct your accounting team to create the smallest financial statement possible. If your income statement has over a hundred lines, it is just too long. Shoot for a more manageable number size, ideally no more than fifty or sixty lines. It's OK if it grows a bit as you do, especially as you add departments. Just don't let it spiral out of control.

To do that, direct your accountants to group related small lines into a single line item. A general rule of thumb is if it is less than 0.5 percent of sales, look to combine it with another line. Take, for instance, travel costs. Sometimes you'll see travel costs broken out like this:

- Air
- Hotel
- Car rental
- And so on

Unless you are doing a huge amount of travel, who cares? If you've budgeted travel costs appropriately, and as long as your team is managing expenses accordingly (and reviewing it in detail quarterly), there is no need to get more granular. When you look at the following examples, it should be intuitive that these line items can be combined to reduce the noise on the income statement. (Do you really need a line on the income statement showing $25 each month for software R&D? I don't think so.)

Example 1

	JANUARY	DECEMBER	NOVEMBER	OCTOBER
Computer and internet (G&A)	273	1,382	984	1,380
Software-ERP (G&A)	180	275	180	180
Software (G&A)	25	25	25	25
TOTAL SOFTWARE	**$478**	**$1,682**	**$1,189**	**$1,585**

Example 2

	JANUARY	DECEMBER	NOVEMBER	OCTOBER
Payroll-Employee Benefits	528	500	637	572
Payroll CPP (68650)	480	454	579	594
Payroll EI (68700)	234	221	282	290
Payroll Expense	18	17	18	19
TOTAL BENEFITS	**$1,261**	**$1,194**	**$1,517**	**$1,476**

Example 3

	JANUARY	DECEMBER	NOVEMBER	OCTOBER
Freight, duty & brokerage (Ops)	25	41	0	66
Freight, duty & brokerage (R&D)	354	21	39	414
TOTAL BENEFITS	**379**	**62**	**39**	**481**

Don't worry, if you are concerned about certain smaller items and how people are spending, you can always ask for detailed reports, in which case your accountants can set up subaccounts to easily run those reports for you with very little extra effort (and add whatever chart line items you'd like to see). Generally, you'll only need to dive into this if your Insights Analysis calls for it. Otherwise, focus your attention on the bigger issues.

☐ **Tick the Box:** You get to tick this box as complete when your income statement is no longer than fifty to sixty lines.

CORE HYGIENE REPORTS

After reviewing the reporting package summary, you may have noticed the reports are set up a bit differently than what normally spits out of the accounting software. I recommend the income statement be presented two ways, and the balance sheet one way (which might be a bit different than what you are used to).

Why? Because these formats provide the sophisticated reader with literally everything they will need. They may (read: will) ask for backup and details, but in terms of high-level reporting, this is the standard you are targeting. Direct your accounting team to set up your financials like the examples shown.

#1. INCOME STATEMENT ACTUAL VS. BUDGET VS. PRIOR YEAR FOR THE MONTH

The following example below only shows the headers and the first few lines of the income statement as an illustration. The full report is available at Entreprenumbers.com.

Month to Date

	ACTUAL	%	BUDGET	%	PRIOR YEAR	%	VARIANCE TO BUDGET	VARIANCE TO PRIOR YEAR
Sales	$241,933	100%	$225,000	100%	$203,218	100%	$16,933	$38,715
Discounts	(3,442)	-1.4%	(3,000)	-1.3%	(2,248)	-1.1%	(442)	(1,194)
NET SALES	238,491	98.6%	222,000	98.7%	200,970	98.9%	16,491	37,521
Cogs								
Materials	102,886	42.5%	90,000	40.0%	83,523	41.1%	(12,886)	(19,363)
Labor	42,271	17.5%	40,000	17.8%	38,215	18.8%	(2,271)	(4,056)
Etc.			...					

While largely self-explanatory, here's the detail:

1. **Actual result for the month.** This is your actual results for the month.

2. **Actual results expressed as a percent of total revenue.** The percent is there for a sophisticated user to see how things are trending relative to sales. If sales are up, it's usually OK if the costs are also up—as long as they aren't up more than sales on a relative basis.

3. **Budget for the month.** This is your budget for the month.

4. **Budget expressed as a percent of total revenue.** Same process as Actual, the percent column is the basis for comparing performance relative to sales. For instance, if sales was 10 percent over budget, a sophisticated user might see the actual labor number (in dollars) is above what you budgeted, but as long as it's the same or lower as a percent of sales, they will recognize that you're managing labor effectively.

5. **Prior year for the same month.** This is your actual result for the same month in the prior year for comparison purposes.

6. **Prior year expressed as a percent of total revenue.** The percentage is used in the same way. To compare results against last year to judge performance on a sales adjusted basis.

7. **Variance to budget in gross dollars.** This is the basis for creating the Top 5 Budget Variance Insights Analysis chart (it's really just the biggest five negative numbers in this column...it's that easy).

8. **Variance to prior year in gross dollars.** Same as above except this is the basis for the Top 5 variance to *prior year* analysis chart. Pick the biggest 5 negative numbers in this column. Also that easy.

#2. INCOME STATEMENT ACTUAL VS. BUDGET VS. PRIOR YEAR ON A YEAR-TO-DATE BASIS

This is the same report as #1, just with year-to-date numbers. That means all the same logic applies. With these reports, a sophisticated user has virtually all the information they'll need to review your information.

#3. INCOME STATEMENT BY MONTH AND YTD

This report shows each month of the current year with a column at the end showing year to date. This report is used by sophisticated users to spot trends and anomalies during the year. It's a detailed and numerical look at the charts you look at every month. Remember, you can pull out any line item here (read: the big expenses) and put them in chart form so you can also stay on top of them. The following example is a shortened version of an income statement showing the headers in the monthly format.

	AUG	SEPT	OCT	NOV	DEC	JAN	YTD
Revenue							
Revenue product sales	106,343	73,705	83,015	107,910	55,124	92,750	518,847
Revenue freight	7,531	4,603	7,715	5,658	4,041	6,923	36,472
Refund product sales	(7,200)	(4,386)	(31,156)	(7,158)	(15,419)	(3,020)	(68,338)
TOTAL REVENUE	**$106,674**	**$73,922**	**$59,574**	**$106,410**	**$43,746**	**$96,653**	**$486,981**

Cost of Goods Sold

	AUG	SEPT	OCT	NOV	DEC	JAN	YTD
Raw materials	41,492	30,946	34,810	28,685	31,667	23,973	191,573
Shopify fees	2,386	1,592	2,583	3,310	2,946	1,958	14,775

#4. BALANCE SHEET BY MONTH AND PRIOR YEAR SAME MONTH

Like the income statement by month, it allows users to spot trends and anomalies. The only difference is that instead of YTD (which wouldn't make sense for a balance sheet), the last column is last year's result for the current month. Again, the following example is a short form of a balance sheet showing the monthly headers.

CURRENT ASSETS	SEPT	OCT	NOV	DEC	JAN	JAN (PRIOR YEAR)
Bank account	10,586	104,362	33,341	(52,573)	(18,262)	(117,101)
Deposit account	2,076	2,076	2,076	2,076	2,076	2,076
Petty cash	476	476	476	476	476	476
1007 PayPal	401	401	401	401	401	401
TOTAL CASH	$13,539	$107,315	$36,294	($49,620)	($15,309)	($114,148)
ACCOUNTS REC	15,3891	23,7687	126,490	301,669	257,622	158,086

☐ **Tick the Box:** You get to tick this box as complete when your main Hygiene reports listed in this section look like the samples here. Reminder: You can download samples of the full report from Entrepreneumers.com.

TO ACCOUNTANTS

This format is often not available in your accounting software. That means you'll have to do some manipulation in order to present statements this way. Yep, it's a bit of a pain in the butt to do it this way. But doing things right isn't always easy, and you want to do things right, right?

If you look around, there are a number of apps (see software section) that can help you automate the reporting process.

REVIEW YOUR CHART OF ACCOUNTS AND FINANCIAL STATEMENT PRESENTATION WITH A CPA OUTSIDE OF YOUR ACCOUNTING STACK (I BET THEY'LL BE IMPRESSED WITH WHAT YOU'VE DONE!)

Your chart of accounts is a blueprint for your financial

statements. When your bookkeeper does a debit or credit, it works its way through the accounting software and ends up on your financial statements. The chart of accounts has a bunch of nerdy complexity to it, complete with master accounts, subaccounts, classes, divisions, locations, etc. It looks something like this in the accounting system:

NUMBER	NAME	TYPE	DETAIL TYPE
1000	1000 Operating Account	Bank	Checking
1001	1001 Space Rental	Bank	Checking
1002	1002 Tax Account Bank	Bank	Savings
1003	1003 Payroll Remittance	Bank	Savings
1004	1004 Projects Deposit	Bank	Savings
1005	1005 Workers Comp Remittance	Bank	Savings

Don't sweat these details; that's for your accounting team to worry about.

Think of the chart of accounts like the electrical wiring schematic for the vehicle. Push this button, and the window goes down. You don't need to know the schematics. You just need to know that if you push that button on your center console, the AC comes on.

In accounting speak, instead of electrical schematics, we have different types of entries (journal entries, transaction entries, etc.). Make a journal entry an entry here, and it shows up in the revenue section of the income statement. Make a journal entry there, and it shows up on the liability section of the balance sheet.

Why is the chart of accounts so (boring and so) important? **Because your entire financial package depends on it,** including all of the analysis that needs to be done to create the simple, intuitive charts to achieve a nine or ten on the empowerment scale. If the chart of accounts isn't right, neither are your charts. If your charts aren't right, there's no way you're at a nine or a ten.

I have good news and bad news.

The *good news* is that, as an entrepreneur, you have zero responsibility to create the chart of accounts. Your accounting team does that when initially setting up your company in the accounting system. It can be adjusted as needed, but really shouldn't be touched very often. Like rewiring a vehicle, it can be done, but you really need to know what you're doing, and if not done correctly, there can be a number of bad, unintended consequences.

The *bad news* is your chart of accounts was likely set up by your bookkeeper. Thinking back to the Accounting Stack, it really should be done by the person responsible for your reporting and compliance function, like your controller. But since you don't have a controller, that means your bookkeeper set it up—who likely doesn't have the proper expertise. They almost certainly used a template from within the accounting software, which may or may not work for your business. Even though you've given your bookkeeper all the detailed instructions that we've covered in this chapter, how can you be sure your chart of accounts is set up correctly?

Simple: you get a second opinion from a CPA outside of your internal accounting department.

I get that some of you reading this will say you don't get much advice or see the value in your current external CPA. If that's the case, maybe it's time to find a new one for this exercise—someone who fits the following two criteria:

- **Experience:** You want a CPA who speaks your language and has experience as a CFO. They should be able to sit you down, review your chart of accounts, and tell you whether it works for a business of your size and type.
- **Industry literacy:** Plenty of external CPAs can help you with your chart review, but not all. Ideally, you want someone in your industry who has worked for, or with, businesses like yours.

When that's complete, congrats! You've got the right blueprints to implement your reporting package.

☐ **Tick the Box:** You get to tick this box as complete when you've had a CPA who fits the criteria above review your chart of accounts and give you the thumbs-up that it's set up correctly.

CHAPTER 13

———

ANNUAL BUDGET

No one likes doing the budget. However, since you obviously *need* a budget, you might as well get your team to do it for you in a format that works for you. If you've never done a budget and/or don't know how to get started, follow these surprisingly simple steps:

1. **Give your accountant a sales forecast by month.** You need to do that; don't expect your accountant to do it. Break it out by segment if you have different products or services with very different margins. If everything is, say, roughly 50 percent gross margin, just give them the overall sales budget by month. No further breakdown needed.

2. **Inform your accountant of any major changes you expect to happen this year.** Examples include hiring staff, letting go of staff, moving offices, adding a product or service, or changing revenue types.

3. **Have your accountant prepare a budget for you.** Nothing for you to do here but set a deadline and wait. Their job is to look at what happened last year, adjust for your sales budget and other expected changes, and deliver you a first version of the budget.

4. **Review the budget.** If you are uncomfortable or don't know how to review a budget, smile broadly and say, "Great job." Now that your statements are broken into accountability areas, you can also push this onto the responsible managers and let them sort it out. Of course, if you have changes to send back, go ahead and get them to do a version two, version three, etc., until you are happy.

5. **Get them to enter the budget into the accounting software so they can drive good reports for you.** This is needed for both the Insights Analysis (budget vs. actual) as well as the core Hygiene reports.

No doubt, you're probably asking yourself, "Is it *really* OK to simply leave it at that?" Yes, it really is.

THE SECRET TO BECOMING A BUDGETING EXPERT

Say this is your first crack at the budget, and you are feeling really uncomfortable with it. Here's what's going to happen for you.

During your new monthly review, imagine you're looking

at the "operating costs" chart and you notice the dotted "actual line" and the black "last year" lines are waaaaay higher than the black "budget line."

Budget Way Off Track

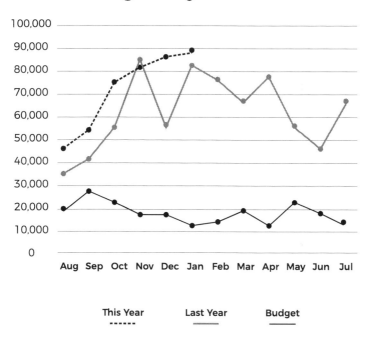

"Why is that?" you ask yourself. Scratch that why-is-that itch. Check in with your accounting team, your head of sales, or your intern with the stolen credit card—whoever it takes to find an answer. Do this enough times, and two things will magically start to happen:

1. Your team will begin to realize you are serious about your budget and about managing your budget. When

it's time to prepare next year's budget, your accountant will likely dig even deeper to develop the most accurate budget possible, leaning on other managers to provide their insight (be it the head of sales or intern with the stolen credit card). You may even find the team wants to do an updated budget partway through the year. That's OK this time, but generally once a budget is set, it should stay set unless there is a really compelling reason to change it.

2. You'll start to be more comfortable understanding what your budget should be and be in a much better position to question the draft budget next year. Don't worry about the quality of the first attempt. It's really just to get the discipline in place and to learn.

Both of these happen naturally IF you are insistent about getting a budget completed each year and making sure the budget lines are included in your charts and you dig into the discrepancies.

You don't need a budgeting lesson to learn how to ask questions. Simply allow yourself to be curious, and you'll be able to (1) identify discrepancies and ask questions, and (2) effectively direct your team to answer those questions. That's all you need to know.

☐ **Tick the Box:** You get to tick this box as complete when your budget is complete, uploaded into your financials, and you are seeing the budget line on your monthly charts review.

CUSTOMIZE AND REPEAT

Over the past few chapters, you've learned all you need to know about financial reporting. Now that you know what you need, your Accounting Stack can take it from here. Just remember, *this has to get done!* If you don't have a solid reporting package, just follow the recommendations in the past few chapters, and you'll be well on your way to a rock-solid financial Hygiene. Once your accounting team can consistently deliver this package in a way that's accessible and easy to understand, you can consider how you might customize your financial report to better suit your industry. Maybe it's time to start diving into more complex Insights Analysis. Perhaps inventory turns by product? Maybe start looking at benchmark analysis comparing yourself against your industry performance.

TO ACCOUNTANTS AND ENTREPRENEURS

Whenever you are asked to send an accounting file to anyone other than your own accounting team, *always send as a PDF!*

Why? Because with an editable format, such as an Excel file, you leave that file open to a deep-diving review. Any sophisticated user will tear that file apart, searching for every error, every mistake, and every issue.

I know this because that's what *I* would do. In fact, that's what we do for every new client that comes to Shift, just so they can see how someone else might tear their financials apart.

CHAPTER 14

TECHNOLOGY AND SOFTWARE

Remember airline travel before web check-in? When you actually had to get to the airport at least two hours before a flight?

- Stand in line forever.
- Talk to the agent while they enter a ridiculous number of keystrokes into their computer.
- Print tickets.
- Head to security (finally!).

The first phase of improvements were kiosks, which drastically reduced lines.

Even better than the kiosk is the web or app check-in option. Follow a couple of links, pick your seat, and the boarding card shows up on your smartphone. When you arrive at the airport, you can walk straight to security and smile politely as they root through your bag looking for whatever innocuous item showed up during screening.

The same advancements apply to software solutions for your accounting department (excluding the pat down). Just like it has with every other industry on the planet, technology has completely disrupted traditional accounting tools and processes. Accountants and bookkeepers have a tremendous range of new programs at their disposal, and yet for many businesses, the adoption of cloud-based and AI (artificial intelligence) tools has been rather slow. It's been slow partly because of the nature of accountants not wanting to change and partly because the technology is still not perfect. With the right procedures to support the gaps in technology, the opportunity is huge.

Despite these slow adoption rates, like online flight check-ins, cloud-based accounting tools will eventually become ubiquitous. Why? Because there are so many advantages. Chief among them are these:

· **Reduction of errors.** Decrease manual entries = reduction of data-entry errors. Especially at the end of a long day.
· **Decreased operating costs.** Connected bank feeds and automated posting rules mean way less bookkeeping time and bookkeeping costs.
· **Low entry cost.** Monthly SaaS fees for most accounting

software are relatively low. You should be in for around $100 per month including related apps. You'll bump above that if you need industry apps or require a true ERP (enterprise software), but $100 should cover most businesses reading this book.

- **More reliable security and storage.** No more worrying about storing all your data on your own little server. These multibillion-dollar companies have more resources to address security and storage needs.

- **Continuous improvements.** New releases are coming out all the time that automatically update when you log in. No need for software updates.

- **Eliminating paper storage.** In the United States and Canada, electronic records are sufficient for audit purposes. All the major cloud solutions have storage of receipts and backup docs (once set up right) so you can toss the paper backup. Many will also store your backup documents for the required seven years, which you can access even if you're no longer a customer (just check the fine print of your software provider). No more filing cabinets full of backup.

- **Industry-specific software.** There are a ton (and growing) of software solutions targeted at operational needs of various industries while automatically tying into the accounting solution. If you check, there will almost certainly be solutions available in your industry.

Automation really is a big deal. In many businesses,

bookkeepers are still required to manually input every transaction. Cloud-based systems make such menial tasks a thing of the past, allowing you to set up "bank feeds" and "credit card feeds" that automatically download your transactions and attach the backup. The business value in potential time savings and error-free automation cannot be overstated, as this side-by-side comparison demonstrates:

THE OLD WAY	THE NEW WAY
Step 1: Put $15 on your credit card buying a coffee for you and a client.	Step 1: Put $15 on your credit card buying a coffee for you and a client.
Step 2: Put the receipt in your wallet.	Step 2: Take a picture of the receipt on an app on your phone and click a couple of buttons to assign to a specific client/job/contract/etc.
Step 3: Forget about the receipt(s) as they pile up in your wallet.	Step 3: Throw away the receipt.
Step 4: Carry around the receipt in your wallet because you keep forgetting to do an expense report.	Step 4: Your bookkeeper logs in and sees that the bank feed matches the photo you took. Clicks one button. Puts feet up on desk in classic bookkeeper triumph pose.
Step 5: Finally empty your overflowing wallet and hand it to your bookkeeper (you don't do your own expenses reports, do you?).	Step 5: Enjoy your coffee and impress your client with your new rapport-building skills.[23]
Step 6: Your bookkeeper prepares your expense report.	
Step 7: Your bookkeeper manually enters your expense(s) into the system.	
Step 8: Your bookkeeper files them in a file folder and puts it in a filing cabinet.	
Step 9: Your bookkeeper waits for the next bank statement.	
Step 10: Your bookkeeper "matches" the receipt to the bank statement and records the entries to match it into the system.	
Step 11: Your bookkeeper hassles you for the expenses on the bank statement that you didn't give him. He quietly curses you. You overhear his silent quiet curse and silently curse him back for being a pain in your ass.	
Step 12: Return to step 10.	

One of those methods is painfully tedious. The other, dare I say it, is *fun*. And who doesn't like fun?

---

23   Or daydream out the window, enjoy a nice walk in the park, or take in a [insert name of favorite team] game.

CHOOSING THE RIGHT ACCOUNTING SOFTWARE

What's the right accounting software for your company? You and your accounting team will have plenty to consider. But first, the obligatory software disclaimer: the names of the software listed in this chapter are for illustrative purposes, not recommendations. We recognize that software changes with time, and newer, better platforms may render the tools I mention here obsolete. As well, the specific needs of your business or industry might dictate one over another.

YOUR MAIN OPTIONS

As of this writing, there are a ton of cloud-based accounting software solutions available to your business. You've likely heard of programs like QuickBooks Online (QBO), Sage, Xero, Freshbooks, Zoho, Wave, Cashhoo, etc. The list goes on. So how do you know what to choose?

GO WITH THE GOLD STANDARD

While it's fine to experiment with software from startups

for some parts of your business, accounting software isn't one of them. Unless you have very unique business needs, I'd suggest going with one of the gold-standard leaders in accounting software. At Shift, all of our accountants only use QuickBooks Online for our clients.[24] There are a few big reasons why.

First, industry leaders have the most resources and evolve their products faster than startups. A lot of startups' sole objective is to gain enough customers to be acquired by one of the big guys. When that happens, there's a good chance that the system as you know it will be significantly changed or even canceled as the larger operation folds the smaller one in. Start by setting up something that will work long-term for you.

The industry leaders (such as QBO and Sage) are built for accountants, whereas some of the startup solutions are often built for solopreneurs to do their own entry (like Xero). Such options are great if you want to do the book-keeping yourself...which you don't. So get a software that works for your bookkeeper. As you scale, it will be easier for your bookkeeper to scale with traditional accounting software. If you are a solopreneur who wants to stay small, this factor isn't nearly as important.

---

24 Think of the Southwest Airlines model; they only have one type of plane, so they only have to train their engineers how to fix one type of plane and train their pilots to fly one type of plane. Same with us; we only have to master one accounting system, which makes it easier to become masters at it.

Industry leaders won't disappear anytime soon. At last check, QuickBooks (Intuit) had well over a billion dollars in cash on their balance sheet, whereas some startups are still burning cash. I'm not saying those startups are going anywhere, but with such an important part of business, I feel better going with a provider with a strong balance sheet (a.k.a., lots of cash!).

When deciding which software is most appropriate for your business, take advantage of as many free trials as you can. When it comes time to pay, the costs are generally reasonable. Don't settle for inferior software just because you shelled out a few bucks for it. There is no harm in trying out a few to see which feels right.

BUT WAIT...THERE'S MORE!

QuickBooks, Sage, Xero, etc., all offer app stores similar to those offered by Apple or Google. These app stores have a wide range of apps (a.k.a. add-ons) that connect to your main accounting software. These apps are designed to (1) address a specific function not handled by the main software, or (2) address the needs of a specific industry. There are a ton of these, and picking the ones right for you can be a bit overwhelming.

In this section, I will walk you through some of the most commonly used features and show you how to pick a good app for your needs. The purpose of this section is to raise your awareness of the possible areas to upgrade and automate your accounting. It is *not* a step-by-step guide to implementing them. That's your bookkeeper's job—to figure out which solution is right for you and implement it. Remember the definition of financial empowerment? Confidently direct your accounting team to get the information you need, when you need it, and in a format that works for you.

RECEIPT AND EXPENSE TRACKING

One of the best and quickest wins you can create for your business is implementing a receipt and expense tracking app. Remember the automation story a few pages earlier about taking a picture of the receipt on an app on your phone? This is what I was referring to.

Here's why this type of app is so great. When set up correctly, receipt and expense tracking apps allow you and your employees to take photos of receipts from a phone (or forward vendor emails with invoices to a unique email address), which then go through an optical reader behind the scenes. A good optical reader will automatically read the date, supplier/ vendor name, the total expense, taxes, payment type, and currency. None of that needs to be data-entered.

The only thing you and your employees (who are incurring

the expense) will have to do other than taking the photos is click a couple of buttons to assign the expense to the right customer or project if the expense is related to a specific client or project (and if it gets charged back to the customer). You'll want to be able to see which of your clients or projects are the most profitable, right?

In literally a couple of clicks, you'll have the best data you've ever had to make decisions. If it's just a general expense, like you buying coffee for the office (because you're a great boss), you don't need to do any extra clicking. Just take the picture and hit submit.

Then, assuming your bank feeds are set up properly (basically, this means your bank statement automatically loads into your accounting software), the app will search the bank feed and "match" any credit card charges or payments from your bank account that match the info picked up by the optical reader.

Now, all your accountant has to do is a quick visual check to make sure everything looks good (remember, the software isn't perfect yet, so a few extra procedures will ensure that you nail it), click a green button, and move on to the next one. Literally, *no more data entry!*

You can even take it one step further and train the software to auto-code certain expenses. Using Starbucks as an example, you can set your software to always code Starbucks to your "Meals and Entertainment" category. That way, your accountant doesn't even have to look at it. You or your employee takes a photo, and that's it. Seriously, it's now posted in your accounting system without another touch.

Some of the most common apps as of this writing are Receipt Bank, Expensify, and Concur, though a whole pile of other options is available. Each program has different functionality. For example, some have an approvals work-flow whereas others don't. Now it's up to your team to select the right software, test, implement, write procedures (see next chapter), and train the users on it.

☐ **Tick the Box:** Consider this task complete when your team has effectively implemented a receipt tracking app and you've personally experienced how much easier life is.

TO ACCOUNTANTS

Be a bit wary of setting up too many auto-post/auto-publish rules. As of this writing, the software isn't totally perfect yet and, depending on what country you are from, the way you want sales taxes handled may not be quite right. The best approach is to leave auto-publish off and, over time, as you notice that one type of expense always seems to be right, click that vendor over to auto-publish. You'll notice that some formats and some vendors always need a bit of tweaking before publishing. Your goal is to get as many vendors set up on auto-publish while still ensuring that the numbers are right.

The other thing to be aware of is the difference between the various apps. Some are very simple, and some are bulkier but have more functionality. Approval workflows is a good example. Some systems have approval workflows built in where a manager can sign off on an employee expense before coming to you. Some don't have that feature, and the expense comes straight to you without any manager approvals. In which case you need really strong processes and procedures (P&Ps)—which we just so happen to talk about in the next chapter. Unless your business is complex with multiple approval layers, I suggest going for a more simplified app (like Receipt Bank) and using P&Ps to address the missing functionality, rather than a more complex software that bogs down the usability.

PAYROLL SOFTWARE

In addition to invoice and receipt tracking, you may also find you need payroll software. Some businesses have a workforce with a mix of salaried, hourly, commission-based employees and/or bonus. For every different way to get paid, there is a payroll platform available to automate calculating deductions and benefits, paying staff, and remitting taxes to the proper tax authorities. They'll all tie into your accounting software and automatically post your payroll journal entries. Most cloud accounting programs have their own payroll module. Start by trying that out, and if you find it doesn't handle your needs, check in with the app store and check out the different solutions.

Your bookkeepers will keep the software current by updating new/terminated employees and changes to comp such as base pay increases and bonuses. For tracking hourly staff, there is also a host of time-tracking apps that help automate this process as well (see next section).

Moving to the right platform will often cost your company far less than outsourcing your payroll needs to a payroll company like Ceridian or ADP.

☐ **Tick the Box:** Consider this task complete when your payroll system is implemented, and your bookkeeper is smiling instead of cursing at payroll time.

TIME TRACKING

The right time-tracking app is critical if your business has one or two scenarios:

1. You have hourly employees.
2. You track time by job or customer/client for billing purposes and/or you need to track time to determine profitability by job or customer.

Using a popular time-tracking app such as T-sheet (owned

by Intuit QuickBooks) or Harvest, your employees can log their time on their phone or computer and allocate their time by hour, by job, by client, or otherwise as needed by your company. Timesheet apps generally have approval processes, so once their manager approves their timesheet, it flows through both for payroll purposes *and* invoicing purposes. Are you a marketing agency that charges employees' time? When someone books five hours to a job, your bookkeeper will see that when it's time to bill the client.

Like receipt and expense tracking, having a strong time-tracking app and related procedures will make sure you're getting the best info possible to increase profitability by understanding which jobs/clients are making money and which ones are not.

The other procedure you'll need is checking that staff are filling out their timesheets properly. Nobody likes doing timesheets, and it's really easy for staff to underreport their hours. (Did Janet really only work seventeen hours this week? Probably not.) No matter how easy the time-tracking app is to use, you'll have to stay on top of the team to actually track their hours.

☐ **Tick the Box:** This task is done when you have a time-tracking app in place, your staff are consistently tracking their hours, and you are using effectively the data (invoicing, labor insights, etc.).

ELECTRONIC PAYMENTS FOR SUPPLIERS AND PAYABLES

If you're still writing checks, then insert dinosaur noises here. Checks used to be ubiquitous, but now they're a thing of the past. Collecting and receiving payment electronically has several advantages:

- No more physical checks—which means no printing them out, and no signing them.
- No more envelopes or stamps.
- The ability to schedule and automate payments.
- The ability to schedule recurring payments.
- The ability to review and approve payments online at any time from anywhere.
- Collect payment from customers.

Your job (or the person you authorize) is to approve payments with the click of a button. Your bookkeeper's job? Figure out which payment processing app to use so that you can do that.

There are a few leading payment processing apps, which

are country-specific based on the rules and regulations of each country. Some worth checking out include Bill.com, Plooto. and Waypay.

☐ **Tick the Box:** Consider this complete when you're no longer signing checks and suppliers are still getting paid.

PERFORMANCE TRACKING

How would you like the peace of mind of knowing your accountants are doing everything they're supposed to be doing—and according to a regular schedule? Good performance or task management software can do exactly that. Shift uses Asana, but there are plenty of options to choose from out there. (More on task management in the next chapter.)

☐ **Tick the Box:** Before ticking this box, make sure you read the chapter on task management. You can tick the box once the lessons from that chapter have been implemented.

BUDGETS AND CASH FLOW

There are lots of cash flow forecasting tools that can help you put together and automate (in part, at least) the cash forecasting process. Beware, accurate cash flow forecasts require extra attention from your team and should NOT rely entirely on the software. The software is really only there to facilitate the process, not to automate away the work of cash flow forecasting.

As for the budget, I'm still a fan of Excel for this. Sure, tools exist, but it's such an involved process with a ton of variables, I haven't seen one yet that is particularly helpful. Overall, I find them clunkier than grinding out a budget in Excel.

☐ **Tick the Box:** When your team has reviewed and selected a tool for this, you can consider it done. Note that they may choose to stick with Excel for this. I'm actually OK with that as long as they've made a legitimate effort testing cash flow and budgeting tools. And, if they choose to stick with Excel, go out and check progress on these apps every year or so...a breakthrough is coming that will replace Excel soon enough.

INDUSTRY-SPECIFIC TOOLS

With a little research, you should be able to find plenty of other software options for some of your more industry-specific needs.

· **Job-costing software.** This is especially helpful to trades or other job-related businesses. These programs can help you through the entire job, from quoting process to invoicing to reviewing profitability by job/client after you're done. These often tie into other apps as well, so your time-tracking app may fit nicely into a job-costing app, whereas some job-costing software has time tracking already built in. A couple of examples are Knowify and Jobber.

· **Quoting software.** This often comes in for any B2B or high-end B2C businesses. Maybe you are a house painter or marketing agency, for instance, and you need to be able to produce reliable, impressive-looking quotes (as in way better than a Word template). In that case, platforms like Proposify offer elegant, customizable quoting solutions that can also tie into your accounting software.

· **Point of sale (POS) systems.** These are tons of options for retail business, allowing greater automation for transactions. These apps can also handle your inventory control, margin by product type, and segment as well. A good POS will allow you to do your sales analytics and dashboard right in the POS software.

· **The list goes on.** Whatever industry you're in, there will be an app for it! Some are more refined, and some are in the new stages. The best way to figure out if there is currently an app out there for you is through trial and testing. If not, check again in a few months. Technology is advancing so quickly that there is an entrepreneur sure to fill that void!

☐ **Tick the Box:** Consider this task complete once you and your team have considered which parts of your business can be automated through technology and you've selected, implemented, documented, and trained appropriate staff on how to use it.

REPORTING SOFTWARE

One frustration I've found with accounting systems is the reporting and dashboard function aren't up to par. There are some other reporting apps, like Fathom, that improve the monthly reporting package, but I still haven't found an existing solution that works. So, we built our own. No, I'm not here pushing my software. I didn't build accounting software or any other apps, because I believe what's out there is as good or better than what most entrepreneurs need. But not the reporting package.

Your reporting app should include all charts, data visualization, and Insights Analysis needed to understand your business in a few minutes or less without having to dig in the details of the financials, while also having all the detailed financial statement reports to satisfy any sophisticated user. If you find a better version than Shift's version, please let me know. I'd love to recommend it!

☐ **Tick the Box:** Consider this done when you've determined your needs, tried as many platforms out as you can, and taken advantage of free trials. No matter what industry you're in, you should be able to find plenty of useful apps. Like the budget and cash flow, for some, Excel is still the best option (if not a bit of a grind).

TO BOOKKEEPERS

This is the number-one place you can upgrade your skills. If you dig in and can master the right software for your company, you will become invaluable to the entrepreneur. It takes some time to understand and learn which ones to choose and how best to implement them. There will be some setback and wrong choices along the way. That's OK. It's all part of the learning process. Your mission is to become an accounting software and app guru to be able to handle anything that comes your way!

THE TAIL WAGGING THE DOG

To be clear, no accounting software out there is perfect. Switching to cloud-based accounting solutions requires careful attention to make sure that (1) it's done correctly, (2) you have the right procedures in place to ensure accuracy and privacy, and (3) your tools are serving *you* and not the other way around. We don't want a "tail wagging the dog" scenario here. In other words, don't bring in a cloud-based accounting app if it's going to mess with your operations. Your operations come first. Your accounting system needs to work around that.

Empower your accounting team to sort everything out for you. Support their work and pay attention when they come back with their findings. Once you've agreed on the right solution, be patient. It can take time to adapt, but once you have, you can't imagine doing it any other way.

Lastly, for those of you who are still nervous about making the switch to cloud-based accounting software, here's my final pitch: you owe it to yourself, your accountants, and your business to at least *try*. Listen to your accounting team's recommendations, download the free trial, and test it out for a month. You can even run the new system side-by-side with the old system during that month to see what works better. Sure, it's extra work, but it will clear your conscience and allow you to make the best decision for your business in the long run. At some point, everything will be cloud-based, except maybe for large complicated businesses. So, you'll have to make the switch at some point.

In the event you don't get your desired result, if the new platforms you've adopted make your accountants' work harder, then reconsider the path you've chosen. The primary purpose of accounting software is to support and service the rest of the business. If the software you're testing doesn't do that, then that's a clear sign you need to try again.

CHAPTER 15

———

PROCESSES AND PROCEDURES

Imagine that your left knee has been bothering you for several months. You can still do most of what you used to, but it feels weaker and a little unstable now. After every run, you find yourself limping a little, though the pain usually goes away after a few minutes.

Lately it's been getting worse, though, and you keep going back and forth about whether to have surgery. Sure, you'd be worse off for a couple of months, but afterward you'd be pain-free and in great shape. That's a lot more appealing than the other option: ignoring the pain, limping around for a while, and hoping that it heals on its own.

But surgery scares you. You've heard the horror stories. What if they perform on the wrong knee? How do you know they'll work on the right (or, in this case, the left) one?

Yes, surgeons have absolutely operated on the wrong knee in the past. That's why when you go in for knee surgery these days, the surgical team will always draw a big X on one knee and an O on the other. Now, operating on the wrong knees doesn't happen anymore.

That's a great example of a simple but effective processes and procedures (P&Ps)—easy to follow, and basically impossible for the surgeon to mess up (picking the correct knee, at least).

Like the rest of your business, your accounting department should have P&Ps in place to give clear directions to staff and avoid making embarrassing mistakes. You never want to find out that you sent the wrong invoice to the wrong customer. It might not be as serious as cutting into the wrong knee, but it's not a good look, and it can negatively impact your business.

This is especially important as staff turns over. When your bookkeeper for the last eight years suddenly ups and leaves for whatever reason, unless the procedures they followed are clearly documented, the next person won't have a clue where to start.

In this chapter, you will learn the necessary framework for making sure your business has the necessary P&Ps, both for the organization as a whole and for your accounting department in particular. Just like surgery, most of us don't want to go through the process of creating P&Ps, even if, once we do, we're always glad we did.

Your P&Ps don't have to be complicated. In fact, they shouldn't be. Clear, straightforward guidelines work best to make sure your accounting team doesn't get their Xs and Os mixed up. When it comes to P&Ps, painfully obvious wins the day—and keeps your business running smoothly even in the face of turnover.

As always, this chapter is not designed to tell you about all the work you should be doing. It is designed to show you all the work you should be *delegating*.

WHAT'S THE DIFFERENCE BETWEEN SOPS, P&PS, AND S&PS?

Before we get too far, I want to make sure we're all clear on terminology.

When it comes to the actual processes that allow business to get done, people use a lot of different phrases. Some refer to them as "standard operating procedures" (SOPs). Some refer to them as "systems and procedures" (S&Ps).

I refer to them as "processes and procedures" (P&Ps).

Why? Because terms like *policy* and *standard operating*

procedure (SOP) make me feel like I'm doing grindy, gross accounting work. Processes and procedures, on the other hand, sound useful (at least to me). After all, no one likes working somewhere where they're overpolicied to death, but everyone *loves* working in a place where the procedures are clear, everyone knows what to do, and no one feels like they're being beaten down with rules.

You're free to call these systems whatever you like. For this chapter—except for a few instances where *policy* really is the appropriate term—I'll be referring to them as P&Ps. Semantics? Maybe. Sometimes semantics help when working on boring accounting topics.

THE BIRD'S-EYE VIEW OF P&PS

Every P&P should have the same basic characteristics:

- P&P name
- Date it was written and approved
- List of procedures
- Who is responsible for each task on the list of procedures
- When the procedure is due, whether fixed date (i.e., by the tenth of each month) or task-dependent (i.e., within two days of receiving an invoice)
- Links to forms as needed
- Examples where helpful

You can certainly make them fancier by including things like revision number, author, approver, etc., but it's not really necessary unless it's required. (It was required in my previous manufacturing business because we were regulated by the FDA.) Adding additional items to the P&P document that aren't required will just make it harder to keep them all current.

THE PRIMARY WORKFLOW

For most businesses, the primary workflow is made up of five basic elements:

1. Prospecting
2. Closing
3. Onboarding
4. Execution

5. Exit

This is your core workflow—your business lifecycle. This flow is fairly self-explanatory for service-based businesses. But even if you're in a highly transactional product business, the flow still applies. Tons of subprocesses help drive this workflow, but these are the main ingredients that make every business go.

Now, you may have noticed that this workflow is not directly related to accounting. So why are we talking about it? Two reasons:

1. Accounting touches each of these core workflows. If the primary workflow processes aren't solid, neither will the interface with accounting be. Having bullet-proof primary workflow P&Ps helps set the standard for your accounting team to follow when creating their own P&Ps.
2. When documenting this workflow, obvious breakdowns in the current way of doing things will show up. Perfect, now your team knows where to focus their efforts in fixing the breakdowns and gaps.

That being said—don't expect your accounting team to take care of your primary workflow. That's the job of your operations manager/director/integrator with support from each divisional leader. Assign the job of documenting all the main workflow procedures to the right people, and make sure it happens. Once these major workflows are documented, you now have the framework of your P&P manual. Most businesses struggle to establish and document their P&Ps, but the businesses that win are invariably the ones that took this step seriously.

ACCOUNTING WORKFLOWS AND POLICIES

Like the core workflows, there are a few key cycles in accounting that need policies and procedures. For simplicity, it's easiest to think about them in three buckets. The following is a *minimum* list of workflows and policies you should have in place in your accounting department.

1. Revenue and collections
   A. Invoicing
   B. AR collections
2. Expenses and payments
   A. PO approval
   B. Invoice approval
   C. Account coding and allocation
3. HR
   A. Employee expense submission and approval
   B. Employee onboarding (from the accounting perspective)
   C. Employee status changes and offboarding
   D. Vacation policy

4. Annual close
   A. Year-end procedures
   B. Taxes
5. Other procedures
   A. Capex
   B. Banking
   C. Industry-specific

Of course, this is not a complete and definitive list. This is really a *minimum* list. You (er, your bookkeeper) can combine or expand these P&Ps as needed for your business. But it's not OK to skip it.

REVENUE AND COLLECTIONS

Guess what happens when you don't have procedures ensuring that your revenue and collections are done right? I don't think "Show me the money that may or may not be missing because I don't have appropriate controls in my business" would have been nearly as famous a movie line.

Invoicing Procedures

With many businesses, invoices only go out because the person responsible keeps breathing down the bookkeeper's neck (usually the entrepreneur). That's clearly a broken way to approach the situation. If the neck breather gets busy, sick, or goes on vacation (or all at the same time), the whole invoicing procedure breaks down. It's time to establish a procedure for making sure your invoices are accurate and delivered on time. Be clear on who is responsible for delivering invoices, and how to make that process efficient.

- Where does the information reside?
- Who is responsible for putting it together?
- What is the deadline for it happening?
- What are the steps?

☐ **Tick the Box:** This procedure is complete when a solid document exists that captures what actually happens during the invoicing cycle.

Accounts Receivable (AR) Procedures

Remember when we talked about the AR and AP reports in chapter 3? Focusing on AR, it's time to decide who is responsible for managing that AR list. Here are some things to think about:

- At what frequency is the AR list being reviewed (weekly, right!)?
- Define the escalation process as receivables go past their due date and get more and more past due. Consider things such as these:
  - Are customers given a reminder when the invoice is due? A second reminder at eleven days?

- What happens if they're delinquent after twenty-two days? Are they cut off?
- How do you communicate with a delinquent customer? A letter? A phone call? A big guy knocking on the door with a bat?
• Define the steps when a payment is received and who is responsible for taking those steps.

I've seen a ton of companies who could solve a good chunk of their cash flow problems with solid AR procedures and execution.

☐ **Tick the Box:** You get to tick this box as complete when you have an AR procedure in place and you're feeling like AR is under control and you don't stress out about it anymore.

TO ENTREPRENEURS AND ACCOUNTANTS

Have you ever wondered why your AP and AR are divided into thirty-day buckets (i.e., the 1–30, 30–60, 60–90, and 90+)? You're not alone. It's one of the great mysteries of accounting. My guess is that some bookkeeper from a hundred years ago decided that's how they were going to do it, and everyone has simply followed their lead ever since.

The problem with the thirty-day buckets is it doesn't tell the real story. They are arbitrary buckets that actually lead to longer outstanding receivables. You don't have to follow the lead of a long-dead bookkeeper At Shift, we use different buckets to encourage faster collections:

- Day 0: Invoice due date.

- Days 1–10 overdue: The "check is in the mail" grace period.

- Days 11–21 overdue: Active and regular follow-up with the client until they pay or commit to when a payment is coming.

- Days 22 and longer overdue: The customer is purposefully withholding money by the time they are three weeks late. It's time to take action on the account. Maybe it's time to withhold future shipments or services until they pay. Maybe their future shipments must be prepaid or, at least, partially prepaid.

- And, if cash flow is tight, we also add another bucket due within the next 7 days. This way, you can call your customer and remind them of the due date and ask if there is any reason why you won't be paid on time. If it's a big number and they are still paying by check, send a courier to pick it up.

These same numbers apply on the AP side too. I generally suggest paying around the twenty-one-day (or even longer) overdue period. Why? A couple of reasons:

1. Paying twenty-one days late improves my own cash situation.

2. It's usually not so late that a tough guy will show up at my door with a lead pipe!

3. It gets vendors used to a schedule that's a bit late, so if I ever actually have a cash flow issue and need to pay five weeks late, it isn't that big a difference from the norm and will be less likely to be a red flag for them.

Of course, paying everything right on time has its advantages too. A long track record of paying promptly will undoubtedly make you a star in the supplier's books, which will make them very likely to be supportive in tough times.

We've found this timeframe works quite well for a lot of entrepreneurs. However, it will almost certainly vary between industries. As always, the point is to find something that works for you.

Purchase Order Approval Policy

OK, here's the first place where *policy* really is the correct word. Assuming your business issues POs, here are some things to be sure are covered:

- Who has the authority to issue purchase orders on behalf of the company?
- Who has the authority to approve purchase orders issues by other staff?
- What are the different purchase levels?
- Do employees with purchase permissions have authority across the board, or only with certain suppliers?
- Does the person issuing the PO also assign account codes and allocations (see more later in the chapter)?

☐ **Tick the Box:** This is complete when your PO approval policy is in place and you actually see approved POs happening.

Invoice and Expenses Approval Process

This is an extension of the PO process. Every supplier invoice and/or expense that comes in (yes: *every**) needs to be reviewed and approved by the person accountable for it. The process should include the following:

- **Routing of information.** When an invoice comes in via email, what happens? Is the bookkeeper or other administration responsible for distributing it to the relevant person for approval? Same thing for invoices coming in by snail mail.

- **Approvals.** Who is authorized to approve what type of expense? For example, the office manager or receptionist can approve all office expenses. The ops manager or assistant office manager can approve all client-related activities. The projection manager must approve plant-related activities.
- **Permissions.** Who is authorized up to what amount? If the authorized person also is responsible for "coding" and allocating the expenses, see next section.
- **Payment.** The other item to consider with expenses is how quickly you want to pay them. Do you want everything paid exactly on time? Do you want to take advantage of any payment discounts? Do you want to pay everything fourteen days late to help cash flow?

☐ **Tick the Box:** Consider this done when you can look at any cost incurred, and your bookkeeper can show you who approved the expenses.

Account Coding and Allocation of Expenses

Basically, this **CRITICAL** procedure ensures that all of your expenses show up in the right spot in the financial statements (a.k.a. financial statement line item) and allocated to the right customer or project (generally called "class," "project," "division," or "customer"). It also outlines who has accountability for making this determination.

For example, say you have an electrical contracting business and you hire a subcontractor to do part of the job. When that subcontractor's invoice comes in, your P&Ps need to outline who is responsible for making sure it lands on your income statement under "COGS—Subcontractors" and allocated to job 5074 (for example).

TO ENTREPRENEURS

DON'T JUST LEAVE THIS TO YOUR BOOKKEEPER! Most entrepreneurs think this is accounting's job. It isn't. Keep reading and you'll see why.

Yes, the coding exercise can be made a lot easier by creating a master list of auto-coded suppliers and eliminating the step altogether for those suppliers. BUT, lots of companies don't do that and then simply push the invoices and receipts to the bookkeeper to code it. The bookkeeper isn't responsible for initiating the expense, though, nor are they responsible for managing the budget around it. Unless they get proper direction, it might not get in the system correctly.

Giving direction for coding is actually the responsibility of whoever is accountable for the expense. I'm NOT saying they have to code it in the accounting software. I'm saying they have to provide that direction to the bookkeeper. The easiest way? Using an invoice and receipt tracking app like we talked about in the software section.

The crux of this P&P is determining who gets responsibility for coding what type of expenses. Sure, the admin costs can likely be handled by your bookkeeper. But what about job costs? That will likely need to be handled by a project manager or ops manager who can allocate the costs between customers or jobs or locations (or whatever the case may be). Your bookkeeper won't have that info unless someone gets it to them. In general, this job needs to fall to the person initiating the expense and/or the person responsible for that line item.

These procedures also need to consider how you receive your invoices (mail, digital, etc.) and what technology you're using to code them (someone writing the code on the invoice dinosaur-style or allocating when capturing it digitally in a program like Receipt Bank). Now when you get your financials, you'll be confident your charts and insights are spot on.

☐ **Tick the Box:** Consider this done when your bookkeeper confirms they aren't left to scramble and code invoices and receipts they know nothing about.

HR PROCEDURES

While most employee procedures are in the HR domain (which often fall to accounting in small businesses), these procedures are focused on how they impact the accounting department.

Employee Expense Submission and Approval

For employee expenses, be sure to clarify:

- In what format do your employees submit their

expenses? Hopefully by now you have them submitting via photo on a mobile app, as you learned in the last chapter.

- How often should they submit them? Weekly? Monthly? It depends in part if employees have expenses that get billed back to clients and, if so, how often you bill clients. If you bill clients weekly, then employees should be submitting expenses weekly. If not, monthly should be fine and it reduces the admin compared to weekly processing.

- How long do they have to submit expense? I suggest a tight policy here. If employees are submitting expenses three to six months after they are done, your numbers will be wrong, especially if it's over a year-end. Not to mention it is a real pain in your bookkeeper's butt to deal with such long-overdue expense reports.

- How quickly will your employees get paid after submission?

- Who has the authority to approve expenses, and what's the process for approval? I suggest the expense approval process be the same as the vendor approval process for simplicity. It might just get routed to a different person (i.e., a manager) for approval.

☐ **Tick the Box:** This procedure is in place when your team can show you the documented procedure and you see it operational with employee expenses.

Employee Onboarding

As it pertains to accounting, what's the process for onboarding employees?

- How do you gather payroll and benefits information?
- What forms need to be filled out based on your local laws and company programs?
- Who's in charge of initiating this process?
- How do they get added to the payroll system?
- Who is responsible for adding them to the payroll system?
- What double-check do you have after the first payroll is done to make sure the new employee was paid correctly? I have seen more than one case where an employee was overpaid for several months before anyone noticed, and (believe it or not) in one case, it was the bookkeeper.
- How are withholding taxes handled? This includes calculating, withholding, and remitting to the appropriate place.

Because the following processes will only happen from time to time, it's doubly important that your team knows exactly how to approach them.

- ☐ **Tick the Box:** This is complete when a documented procedure is in place and it works with the next team member onboarded.

Employee Status Changes and Offboarding

Similar to onboarding, this procedure ensures that changes in employee pay, either up or out, get handled. Things to consider include the following:

- Who initiates the process?
- What changes to employee status are being made?
- Who approves the change in status?
- Who is responsible for updating the payroll system?
- What changes need to be made in the payroll system?
- If an employee quits or is terminated, what compliance or government forms need to be complete?

☐ **Tick the Box:** Same as employee onboarding, this is complete when a documented procedure is established that works with the next employee status change.

Vacation Policy

Now for the questions on every employee's mind:

- What is your vacation policy?
- How do you track who is entitled to what vacation allowance?
- How do you track vacations as they happen?
- What is your policy for rolling over vacations if people don't take them?

And since your vacation policy has to meet the required employment standards where you operate:

- Who is responsible for ensuring that you are meeting the required employment standards?

☐ **Tick the Box:** This is considered complete when your documented policy is complete, signed off by you, and circulated to all staff so there are no questions or confusions.

OTHER PROCEDURES
Capital Expense Policy

Here is another place where policy is essential. Especially for those in manufacturing (or other capital-intensive businesses), it makes sense to have a policy in place for delegating authority on capital expenses.

- Who has the authority to make these decisions at what purchase values? For example:
  - Managers can authorize up to $5K items.
  - Directors can authorize up to $25K.
  - The executive team can authorize up to $50K.

Those values are simple examples. Set whatever value makes sense for you and your business. The clarity will set you free!

☐ **Tick the Box:** As always, this is complete when a documented procedure is in place and you see it functionally working.

Year-End Processes

What are the procedures related to those external CPAs we discussed in chapter 1? You don't want to wait for your CPAs to call you to set up your year-end review. It's better to be proactive. Create procedures for the following questions:

- When should you reach out to your accountants for quotes each year?
- When should you set your review period?
- What working papers should be prepared and handed to the external accountants before they ask for them? (Done right, this can save you money on your review... external accountants love organized businesses.)

Take this same approach with benefits renewal (both liability and benefits) and any other activities that happen on a yearly basis (for more on this, see the next chapter on task management) as well.

☐ **Tick the Box:** This is complete when a documented procedure is in place and working effectively.

Banking Procedures

If you have any bank loans, you'll likely have some monthly and annual reporting due to them. Be sure to capture everything that needs to be sent to them.

- Financials
- Margin report
- Covenant calculations
- Etc.

Once this procedure is in place, your bookkeeper will be ahead of your banker by getting them all the required information without being asked, so you're on top of things. If you're having a tough stretch financially, showing you're proactive and organized will definitely help with the relationship.

If fact, if you have some bad months, it would be a good idea to add a step in this process for your bookkeeper (or you if they don't have the skill) to add a note to the banker, recognizing things aren't on track and what you're doing to get things back on track.

☐ **Tick the Box:** This is complete with a documented procedure and you see your banking information seamlessly being sent to the banker each month.

Business-Specific Requirements

What about your business license or other business-specific requirements? For example, if you are a real estate broker, you might need to submit a compliance document every month. Who handles that? *When* is it handled? What other industry-specific or professional organizations have annual actions that can't slip through the cracks? Are there other unique needs of your business? This is the time to direct the team to start documenting those procedures, as well.

REVISE, REVISE, REVISE

P&Ps are all about knowing *who's* responsible for *what* at all times. When you're deciding on the *who,* remember to use job titles, not names. The job of processing invoices doesn't go to Peggy, for instance; it goes to the bookkeeper. Sticking with job title ensures that you don't have to change up all your documents when people leave or change roles.

Things change every year. Companies grow and shrink,

roles are split and consolidated, and people come and go. Your P&Ps should always reflect the *current* state of operations at your business, so be sure to review and update them regularly. By that, I mean reviewed at least once per year.

Again, this isn't all on you. When it comes to P&Ps, all you should have to do is direct the right people to get it done and then sign off on their work. When given the right attention, P&Ps help your business run smoothly without requiring you to field a thousand questions every day. When your team is empowered to find the answers and do the job themselves, you'll be free to give your attention to other areas of your business.

TO BOOKKEEPERS

Heads up, unless you work for a rare breed of entrepreneur–we're talking the unicorn of entrepreneurs here–who loves procedures, every time you raise this subject, the entrepreneur will usually run screaming for the door for an urgent appointment they just happened to remember at that moment. As much as most entrepreneurs hate process, they will appreciate your efforts. It's totally worth it, and you'll be a hero once things start flowing smoothly.

Stick with it. Some people find it's best to knock off a procedure every week or two, whereas some like doing a procedure-writing blitz. Either way is fine. Just get them down and go pick up your victory belt from HR.

CHAPTER 16

———

TASK MANAGEMENT

Task management is the living extension of the processes and procedures from the last chapter. Documented procedures sitting on your server are almost certainly going to be ignored. When built into easy-to-use task management systems, they come alive, making sure your business is running smoothly. When you have a solid task management process (with the appropriate technology supporting it), you'll never be able to live without it again.

For many entrepreneurs, the very thought of task management can lead to feelings of stress and anxiety. We lose sleep not because we don't know what needs to be done, but because we have so much uncertainty not knowing if everything that is *supposed* to get done *actually* gets done. You *hope* your team is doing its job, but *hope is not a strategy*. At least, not a good one.

When you have a good system in place, that feeling goes away—replaced by good, old-fashioned empowerment. Instead of lying in bed wondering whether important tasks are getting done, you're celebrating all the free time you have thanks to your efficient system and automated reports letting you know everything is on track.

TASK MANAGEMENT ESSENTIALS

In any business, you have tasks that need to be completed daily, weekly, monthly, quarterly, and/or annually. Accounting is no different. In fact, accounting was *made* for checklists. Aside from dealing with occasional curve balls, emergencies, and first-time financing applications, accountants have a highly consistent routine from day to day, month to month, and year to year.

All of the P&Ps we discussed in the last chapter need to live inside a task list somewhere, and that task list needs to live in a task management or project management software.

You should have a distinct task list for each of the following:

1. **Daily activities.** For things that need to happen every day, like bank deposits and processing receipts.
2. **Weekly activities**. For things that only happen weekly, like invoicing (assuming your procedure is to invoice weekly).

3. **Monthly activities.** For month-end close procedures, employee expenses, etc.
4. **Quarterly activities.** For the reports or activities that are required quarterly.
5. **Annual activities.** Year-end time. Since these only happen once a year, it's easy to forget all the tasks. Record them, being prompted by the system when it's due (or, better yet, coming due).
6. **Payroll activities.** One of the few accounting tasks you really can't mess up in the business without a parade of angry employees at your door. These don't fall into the other task cycles, as payroll is typically done either biweekly or semimonthly.

The following sample monthly task lists show exactly what I mean. Keep in mind that, just as in previous chapters, the following example is meant to be an illustration. You (read: your bookkeeper) will have to update each task list to fit your business. There are tons of samples online you can draw on to shortcut the process for yourself. These tasks, of course, live in your task management software.

TASK	OWNER	NAME[25]	DUE DATE
Complete bank rec in QuickBooks Online	Bookkeeper	Peggy	Oct. 6
Process expense reports for approval	Bookkeeper	Peggy	Oct. 4
Approve expense reports	Director of Ops	Susan	Oct. 6
Pay approved expense reports	Bookkeeper	Peggy	Oct. 12
Process monthly Amex credit card payment	Bookkeeper	Peggy	Oct. 12
Process monthly Mastercard credit card payment	Bookkeeper	Peggy	Oct. 22
Review and process manual journal entries	Controller	James	Oct. 9
Setup/review recurring monthly journal entries	Controller	James	Oct. 9
Complete balance sheet reconciliations	Controller	James	Oct. 10
Complete fixed asset amortization schedule and entry	Controller	James	Oct. 10
Update accruals schedule and book/update entry	Controller	James	Oct. 10
Review bookkeeper's work	Controller	James	Oct. 8
Fund and complete monthly corporate tax installments	Bookkeeper	Peggy	Oct. 15
Complete monthly charts	Controller	James	Oct. 11
Complete monthly Insights Analysis charts	Controller	James	Oct. 11
Complete Insights summary	Controller	James	Oct. 11
Create and preview month-end reporting package	Controller	James	Oct. 11
Deliver report to owner	Controller	James	Oct. 12
Save monthly report on Google Drive	Controller	James	Oct. 12
Complete and submit bank margin report	Controller	James	Oct. 20

---

25 In the Processes and Procedures section, we talked about not using names, but roles. In this case, you'll want to have the right person's name attached to the task to make things clear and easy. A good task management tool can help you handle any changes in HR. If Peggy leaves and you hire a new bookkeeper, just reassign Peggy's tasks and you're good to go.

TASK MANAGEMENT MUST-HAVES

Not sure what you need in a good task management system? There are many different platforms out there, each with their own bells and whistles. At minimum, look for a system that both is simple for staff to use and also has automated reporting and dashboards that allow you to see which projects are on track. Depending on your own needs, you may need one that also has dependencies (i.e., when a task is checked off as being done, the next task is initiated). Some common ones out there are Asana, Basecamp, Wrike, and Trelllo.

☐ **Tick the Box:** Consider your task management in place when your accounting team has their daily, weekly, monthly, quarterly, and annual tasks loaded into a task management tool and you're getting regular reports on how well they are knocking off their tasks.

TO ENTREPRENEURS

Speaking of yearly activities, why do you need a year-end, anyway?

In reality, you might not need one. While you're legally required to file your taxes, you're not legally required to perform a year-end review. Many businesses run year-ends simply because they think it's mandatory, often spending a few grand to get it done. You may be required to do it from a lender or business partner if you have investors. But otherwise, it is optional. While it does have its benefits–for instance, it's a great way to confirm that you meet compliance guidelines–you may not need it. If you are confident that your business is compliant, or if you otherwise feel that your year-ends aren't helping you, skip them and save the money.

These year-end reviews fall into one of three categories:

1. **Audits.** The highest level of year-end review. You're probably not doing this as it's generally done only by public companies or larger companies with special requirements.

2. **Review Engagement.** Less intensive than an audit, more work than a Notice to Reader. This is often required by a bank or lender depending on size of loan.

3. **Notice to Reader.** The least invasive and cheapest of year-end reviews, this involves some basic compliance work and you get a shiny set of financial statements on your accountant's letterhead.

So, why are you doing a year-end?

NOW THAT'S GOOD HYGIENE!

That's the Hygiene Roadmap. In this part, you learned:

- How to direct your accounting team to create a reporting package you are confident in.

- How to adopt the tech and software tools that are right for your business.
- How to establish clear policies and procedures that outline how your business should run.
- How to document and track all your tasks in a task management system that tells you whether your team is current, ahead, or behind.

Put that all together, and you've got some damn good Hygiene.

TO ENTREPRENEURS

You're not an accountant, and you may have a hard time knowing if your bookkeeper is doing a good job. There are some technical skills, like accrual accounting, that a lot of bookkeepers miss. You may not know if they're missing it or not. I get it, and that's OK. See the next chapter for some guidance on how to tell if your bookkeeper is strong enough to go on this journey with you.

CONCLUSION

IS YOUR TEAM UP FOR THE JOB?

That it's for *Entreprenumbers!* If your accounting team can execute the processes outlined in this book, I guarantee you will have solved the majority of your accounting pain.

To recap, here are the four things I hope you take away from this book:

1. **It's time to change your relationship with your books.** Turn accounting from a source of pain into a source of power.
2. **Know the distinction between Hygiene (not for you) and Insight (for you).** Think of Hygiene as a lump of coal and Insight as a diamond. One is the raw fuel that makes your business go, and the other is the beautiful gem that raw material can produce.

3. **Your monthly reporting package can work for everyone.** It reports on both the Insights for you and Hygiene for sophisticated users.
4. **All of this can be done quickly, simply, and intuitively**...without ever having to look at your financial statements.

Now that you understand what needs to be done, all that's left is to hand this book off to your accounting team to have them execute it. At this point, you'll have to ask some hard questions. Is your accounting team up for the job? Do you even *have* an accounting team?

Compared to big business with large budgets who can afford a whole army of sophisticated financial employees, entrepreneurial businesses tend to be a little leaner. You likely don't have a full Accounting Stack like the one described earlier in the book. You probably only have a bookkeeper or a single in-house accountant at most.

I hate to be the bearer of bad news, but if you attempt to go down the road I've mapped out in this book, your bookkeeper or accountant might not be able to come with you.

Here are five questions to ask your bookkeeper to see if they are even ready to *start* this journey. Don't worry if you don't understand what you're asking. Just ask the following questions and look for answers similar to the ones provided here.

QUESTIONS FOR YOUR BOOKKEEPER

"PLEASE SHOW ME THE LATEST BANK RECONCILIATION."

Regardless of whether you are using a cloud-based accounting system or an old-school desktop version, they should be able to show you the latest back rec is complete and balanced. If it's before the tenth of the month, it's fine if they show you the previous month if they are still working on closing the current month. If they produce it, that's a good sign. If not and they start making a bunch of excuses, it's a big, big red flag. The bank rec is accounting 101, and they should be all over it.

"ARE WE ON ACCRUAL ACCOUNTING OR CASH BASIS ACCOUNTING?"

Another question you can ask is "Please show me the revenue accruals for the past few months."

An accrual is an accounting thing that helps the statements more meaningful versus cash basis where revenue is only recording things when the cash comes in. This is most relevant for companies whose services stretch over months. For example, you get a $100,000 contract with a 50 percent deposit from your customer. When you complete the work three months later, you get the other 50 percent.

In cash basis accounting, you'd record revenue 50 percent when the deposit hits the bank and 50 percent when the balance hits the bank. In accrual accounting, you'd record the revenue based on when you *earned* it, not got paid for it. This means you wouldn't record either the deposit or the final payment as revenue. Say you did work in each of the three months following the deposit; you'd record the revenue one-third per month in those working months. The following chart may help clarify:

MONTH	EVENT	REVENUE USING CASH BASIS ACCOUNTING	REVENUE USING ACCRUAL BASIS ACCOUNTING
March	50% deposit paid	$50,000 recorded as revenue	$0 (assuming no work is done)
April	25% of the work is complete	-	$25,000 recorded as revenue
May	42% of the work is complete	-	$42,000 recorded as revenue
June	33% of the work is complete	-	$33,000 recorded as revenue
July	Final 50% balance paid	$50,000	-

If they haven't done any accruals, that's a huge red flag (especially if your business has jobs that span across months). If they bring you a list of them (they may take a moment to prepare the list for you), then it's a good sign they have the basics in place.

"PLEASE SHOW ME THE PREPAID AMORTIZATION SCHEDULE."

Like accruals, they should have a list of expenses that are

paid once for the year that they "amortize" over the rest of the year. For example, if you pay your insurance premium in one shot for the year and it's $8,400 for the year, rather than expensing the $8,400 in July when it was paid, it should be set up on a prepaid schedule and expensed $700 ($8,400/12) each month. If your team isn't doing that...red flag!

"PLEASE SHOW ME A CHART OF OUR GROSS MARGIN FOR THE PAST TWELVE MONTHS."

If your business is relatively consistent, your margin should be too. If the gross margin line looks like a mountain range, something probably isn't quite right, and they likely aren't doing the basics right.

"SHOW ME THE PROFITABILITY BY SERVICE/PRODUCT TYPE."

However you naturally think of the different lines of your business, ask your accountant to show you the profitability by each of those lines of business.

If they haven't set up the books in a way for you to measure that, it's a sign they might (read: will) have a tough time implementing the learnings in this book. It's a reasonably simple request that should already be in place.

DO THEY HAVE TO NAIL EVERY QUESTION?

They don't have to pass all five questions above with flying colors. This is just a quick-and-dirty exercise to see if they are a clear no.

I don't say this to badmouth anyone. I have seen some great bookkeepers in my day. I've seen some great accountants fighting the good fight for their entrepreneurs. But even the good ones might not be up to the tasks outlined in this book. It's simply not what they were trained to do.

If that's the case, you have two options. The first is to do whatever you can to bring them along for the ride. At Shift, we operate under the assumption that skills are secondary to cultural fit. If you love your bookkeeper, but they lack some of the essential skills I've outlined, either train them or redefine their role. If you have a wonderful accountant who isn't up to Insights Analysis but great at everything else, simply find someone else who can handle the Insights part. There may be some additional associated costs, but that overall cost will be less of a pain than completely changing out your team.

The second option is to outsource.

IS OUTSOURCING RIGHT FOR YOU?

If you don't have a strong accounting team—or if you

don't have an accounting team at all—you may not need to hire and train one in-house. An entire industry of outsourced accounting solutions has emerged, powered by rapid advances in technology and a shifting business environment.

Outsourced options allow you to better serve your needs at a greater value. Instead of paying for a full-time bookkeeper, you're potentially paying roughly the same (depending on biz size, complexity, etc.) for the *full* Accounting Stack. Outsourced, you're getting *part* of a bookkeeper, *part* of a controller, and even a bit of the CFO. A business doing under $10 million may not necessarily need any of these roles full-time, but it definitely does need a bit of each.

If you do decide to outsource, make sure you do your due diligence. Please. Just because a firm has been around for many years, that doesn't mean you should trust them. There are plenty of accounting firms out there who have been doing things the wrong way for a hundred years. That's not who you want to hire. Here are a few things you should ask of your outsourced accounting firm.

"WHAT ARE THE CREDENTIALS OF MY LEAD ACCOUNTANT?"

I remember one time in the early days of Shift, I was on LinkedIn looking to poach accountants from a well-known competitor. Clicking their profiles, however, I was shocked to find that one of the candidates—who was a lead accountant at that firm—had previously been a barista at Starbucks before becoming lead accountant. And that was the *most senior job* on their entire resume.

This isn't to knock baristas. Food-service workers have more complicated and demanding jobs than many of us give them credit for. However, those jobs have nothing to do with accounting. The Hygiene and Insights Roadmaps are equal parts art and science. No matter how well a Starbucks barista has been trained, they won't have the deep knowledge of how to balance the art and science of accounting to deliver the information you need, when you need it, and in a form you can understand.

"PLEASE SHOW ME YOUR MONTHLY REPORTING PACKAGE." (DOES IT HANDLE BOTH HYGIENE AND INSIGHTS?[26])

Ask to see an example of their monthly reporting package. Not only do you want a firm to deliver good Hygiene, but you want it delivered in a way that makes sense for you. If you can't make heads or tails out of what you see, then run far, far away.

Same with Insights. Are they just giving you the standard

---

26 "Hygiene" and "Insights" are words we use at Shift, not industry-standard terms. If they have their version of Hygiene and Insights and call it something different, that's fine, as long as you can see a package that addresses both sides of the reporting package.

reports out of the accounting system, or are they actually delivering Insights that will help you make better decisions for your business?

"HOW DO YOU HOLD US (THE CLIENT) ACCOUNTABLE?"

One key skill in a successful outsourcing relationship is the ability to hold the client accountable. What happens if your team stops submitting receipts? What happens if your team isn't filling out their timesheets correctly? A good outsourcer should have a solid (you guessed it) procedure for dealing with clients who are not doing their part in the relationship. Same thing goes for requests that are out of scope.

"PLEASE SHOW ME YOUR P&P LIBRARY."

Ask to see their P&P library. A good outsourced accounting firm should have an entire library of policies and procedures. Say you're missing a vendor invoice approval policy. The firm should be able to pull that P&P from their shelves, tweak it for your business, and provide it to you. Expect to receive a P&P manual very quickly after starting with an outsourced accounting company. If you don't, get out while you still can.

TAKE YOUR PICK

Picking the right outsourced solution can take you from whatever state of disempowerment you are at today and get you fully empowered over a few months. Be sure to be fair and give your new provider time to get up to speed and implement the appropriate changes. You also have to do your part.

We've learned there are a few keys to getting yourself ready for outsourcing. Yes, picking the right provider is critical, but so is being ready. Here are a few things you can do to be sure you are ready for a successful outsourcing relationship:

- **Have a lead internal point of contact who is *not* the entrepreneur.** If you are going to be the lead contact person for your outsourced team, you're likely going to be the bottleneck and mess it up. Make sure you have an ops manager or office manager who can chase up the missing info the accountants need.
- **Be clear on how far behind your books really are.** We've seen clients who showed up two years behind in their books. That's OK. Just be honest with your outsourcer, so you don't start on the wrong foot.
- **Make sure you have your ops software dialed.** Your accounting solution should be able to implement processes and procedures around the software you currently use for your ops. Don't change ops systems for your accountant. It might screw up the rest of your business.

- **Only proceed if you have in-house discipline for P&Ps.** If you know your team is not disciplined at following P&Ps, chances are outsourcing accounting will be a fail. Success *requires* discipline from your staff to follow procedures that touch the accounting function.
- **Consider your growth rate.** Outsourcing is a great way to support you during a growth phase of your business. But, if you're doubling every six months, it might be a bit too fast for your outsourcer to keep up with and/or you just might need someone in-house.
- **Get rid of the administration.** Accounting and administration are two very different things. A good accountant doesn't want to also handle your admin tasks (like ordering office supplies and opening mail). Likewise, a good administrator might not be a good accountant. Only proceed if you can separate these tasks and let your outsourced accountant focus on accounting.

I encourage you to use this information to find someone who has the most robust program, process, and results out there. In my admittedly very biased opinion, I think Shift is the best in the business. However, if you can find someone better, then by all means, go with them. If you can't, give us a call.

Otherwise, thank you very much for reading, and I hope you enjoyed this book!

LOOKING FOR SOME FREE RESOURCES?

If you're feeling stuck and looking for help get you going, head to Entreprenumbers.com for some free tools and resources.

APPENDIX

DASHBOARD ANALYSIS

The dashboard in your car is obviously a critical tool. With just a glance, you know exactly how the basic systems in your car are functioning (speed, fuel, distance, etc.) and whether anything needs your attention. Sure, the dashboard may not tell the whole story—you still have to check under the hood and have your car serviced every now and then—but if all the indicators are good, you can be reasonably confident your car is healthy.

Financial dashboards work the same way. By accessing a small set of key metrics, you will always know exactly how your business is running.

A TROPICAL-ISLAND STATE OF MIND

You can always tell an entrepreneur on vacation. They're the ones pacing around and constantly checking their phones to see whether everything is running smoothly back home. Forget the miles of pristine beach sprawling out in every direction. All these entrepreneurs are concerned about are the latest numbers as they brace themselves for the worst, annoying their significant other in the process.

Of course, ignoring your phone is easier said than done. If you're really going to enjoy yourself, you need peace of mind. That's precisely what the dashboard offers you. The goal is a "Tropical Island" dashboard: a set of no more than five metrics that you absolutely need to know in order to enjoy the rest of your day phone-free. A dashboard with twenty metrics isn't a dashboard at all; it's a report.

SOME STARTER METRICS

If you don't have a dashboard and don't know where to start, try these:

1. Sales Growth
2. Quality of Growth
3. Operational Efficiency
4. Customer Satisfaction
5. Future Sales Pipeline

METRIC 1: SALES GROWTH

Most entrepreneurs are growth-minded. If you're reading this book, then for sure you are. Some considerations to make sure your accounting team has set this metric up properly:

- Should your growth be set up annually, quarterly, or monthly? Generally, the faster your growth, the narrower your window for measuring it.
- Is your business seasonal? If so, you might want to view your growth year over year or quarter over quarter, since monthly comparisons won't be as helpful.

Set a target sales growth, and then in two seconds you can see if things are on track or not from a sales perspective.

METRIC 2: QUALITY OF GROWTH

This metric will show you whether the growth is good growth or the right kind of growth. Growing with the wrong type of product or customer is often the biggest mistake an entrepreneur can make. Here you'll be selecting a metric such as contribution/margin/profit by customer, project, job, or product line. Your accounting team can sort out the details, but your goal is to confirm your growth is healthy. Unless you have a strategic reason, there's little point in growing a segment of your business that is unprofitable in the long run.

For example, let's say you have a construction business that specializes on new homes and renos. When examining the metrics, you discover that your new homes are generating a 15 percent gross margin, but your reno division (for a bunch of reasons) is only generating a 6 percent gross margin. If that's my business (remember, I've owned a construction business), I'd set my dashboard metric to be "margin on new business sold" and set the minimum target at 15 percent. That way, your sales team will be focused on new homes (which is already running at 15 percent) and either eliminating or repricing the renos. New homes at 15 percent = good growth. Renos at 6 percent = bad growth.

METRIC 3: OPERATIONAL EFFICIENCY

How do you know if your business is running smoothly?

If you're a service provider, you might look at on-time delivery or labor efficiency. If you're selling products, you might look at the number of rejected or low-quality products. Whatever the case, work with your team to figure out the number-one indicator to determine if your operations are running effectively.

METRIC 4: CUSTOMER SATISFACTION

Checking in with your customers and knowing they are happy is one of the best sleeping pills an entrepreneur can take. The most common customer satisfaction metric is a net promoter score (NPS). You've almost certainly been surveyed using this method, even if you didn't realize it. In a basic NPS approach, customers can be asked a variety of questions, with the key question being:

On a scale of one to ten, "How likely is it that you would recommend this company/service/product to a friend or colleague?"

Obviously, the higher the number, the better. There's more to NPS than this, but the nuances of this conversation are beyond the scope of this book. Besides, there's a ton of info about NPS online, so feel free to explore further there while we move on to...

METRIC 5: FUTURE SALES PIPELINE

With this, you can determine whether you have enough in the sales pipeline to continue growing your business and sustaining that growth. You might measure it as thirty-two prospects in the pipeline, or $287,000 of deals in the hopper. Either way, if you assign a percentage-based estimate of the likelihood of a close based on the stage of the sales cycle (plus a "gut" factor if applicable), you (er, your accountant) can multiply the deals in the pipeline by their respective and expected close percentages to figure out how much sales you expect to generate based on the current pipeline.

Once you get comfortable with this metric, you'll start to find yourself feeling confident or frightened by the future. Hopefully it's the former, but either way, you'll have clarity on the future. If you are set up and hit your targets for all five of these metrics, you'll know that you're growing, growing well, running well, keeping your customers happy, and working toward a bright future. Now, back to your tropical island!

MEASURE, MODIFY, REPEAT

Now that you have a starting point for your five metrics, here's what to do:

1. Direct your team to create a dashboard with these five metrics.
2. Track them religiously.
3. Modify as needed. Over time, you may find that some metrics are more helpful than others. You may even find that some are no help at all. Not a problem—every business is a little different. These metrics are simply the minimum starting point for your business. As soon as something doesn't work, just evolve as you need to according to your needs and industry.
4. As you evolve, consider whether each metric needs to be measured daily, weekly, monthly, and so on. If you operate a call center, for instance, one good metric might be number of calls per day. If you operate a job placement service, you may want a monthly metric of

positions filled. Whatever the case, the frequency of your measurements should vary. At minimum, I would recommend having at least a couple of them being measured weekly.

WATCH OUT FOR UNINTENDED CONSEQUENCES

Andy Grove, Intel's co-founder and former CEO, as well as *Time*'s 1999 "Man of the Year," knows a thing or two about metrics. Grove once famously said, "For every metric, there should be another paired metric that addresses adverse consequences of the first metric."[27]

In other words, working to improve results in one area may produce unexpected damaging results in another. For instance, say you're trying to push labor utilization up. Your success might bring unintended consequences—namely, burned-out staff and a lower quality of work as your workers scramble to get their numbers up.

You can never avoid adverse consequences entirely, but you can try to anticipate them. For each of your key metrics, work with your accountants and department heads to consider what these adverse metrics might be and start measuring.

---

27   Google tells me that this quote is indeed attributed to Andy Grove, and there are plenty of sources to back this up. However, the sources are always secondhand. It's someone quoting Andy Grove (like I am here), rather than Andy himself saying it. So Andy, if you didn't say this, sorry to put words in your mouth!

ACKNOWLEDGMENTS

A huge thank-you to a small hoard who have made this book possible. Some of you helped me directly with this book, and some of you helped in life.

Either way, I am eternally grateful to Sandy and Marlee Sheinin (my parents), who have stood by all of my crazy business and athletic endeavors. My sister and brother-in-law for not only being one of Shift's first clients, but for always being there for solid ideas, dinners, and a good laugh.

Anna Jean-Louis for trusting me enough to be Shift accountant #1. The entire Shift team who are such a great group of people.

Tao Forum for over a dozen years of amazing meetings and experiences. A ton of EO members I've met over the years who have helped me navigate entrepreneurship.

All the Shift clients who have trusted us with their books.

Chas Hoppe for hours of time going back and forth with my crazy edits.

Shannon Johnston for continuing to encourage me and surprise me with your capabilities.

ABOUT THE AUTHOR

In the late 1990s, at the age of twenty-five, **SPENCER SHEININ, CPA, CA,** came to the life-changing realization that he was an entrepreneur stuck in the body of an accountant/investment banker. Breaking free from the career path he was on, he went on to own several businesses in industries including manufacturing, construction, cold storage logistics, and real estate.

Spencer is now the founder and CEO of Shift Financial Insights, providing ridiculously simple accounting and financial insights for businesses on the rise. Guided by the belief that entrepreneurs can change the world, Shift is on a mission to help small and medium-sized businesses by removing their financial blind spots and turning the numbers side of the business from a source of pain to a source of power!

Spencer is a highly rated international speaker, delivering engaging and actionable keynote presentations and workshops to industry and membership associations such as the Entrepreneurs' Organization (EO) and The Executive Committee (TEC). (For speaking inquiries, please visit www.shiftfinancial.co/speaking.)

Using the same drive in sport as he does in business, Spencer is a passionate endurance athlete and has completed several marathons, ultramarathons as far as 100 miles/160 kilometers, Iron Man, distance cycling events, and a marathon distance swim.

Spencer lives in beautiful West Vancouver, Canada.

Manufactured by Amazon.ca
Bolton, ON

32253788R00152